Outside
IN SHORTS

Scott — I hope you enjoy a few of these stories. Cheers to writing a couple of your own as you chase parts unknown!

Outside
IN SHORTS

Seasons of Life, Luck, and Loss in the Outdoors

by
Allen Crater

Copyright © 2022 by Allen Crater

All rights reserved. No part of this book may be reproduced, scanned, or distributed in any printed or electronic form or through any media or platform without written permission from the author.

All artwork by Chris Conran and may not be reproduced without the artist's permission.

Some stories previously appeared in the following publications:

"Parts Unknown"	*Backcountry Journal*
"Sawtooth"	*Backcountry Journal*
"Season's End"	*Solace*
"Five Loaves and Two Fishes"	*Fly Fusion*
"Echoes of the Forest"	*Strung*

"The World Is Too Much With Us" by William Wordsworth (1770-1850) in public domain.

Cover design by Chris Conran

ISBN: 979-8-407-54834-8

Contents

Foreword	1
Solace in the Solitude	4
Spring	
Fishing Miracles	9
The Preservation of Fire	19
Can't Be Done	22
The River Gives	27
A Day on the Water	30
The Best Water Still Lies Ahead	34
Summer	
The Last Frontier	45
Bonds of the Wild	57
Taking the Bronze	60
Going Native	63
River Thoughts	76
Sawtooth	79
Parts Unknown	86
Lucky Hats	91
Five Loaves and Two Fish	95
Return to Wind River	106

Fall
   An Ode to Shastaland   115
   The Lessons of Silver Creek   121
   Yellowstone   124
   Michigan Escape   131
   My Uncle's Farm   134
   Echoes of the Forest   139
   Pink Cake   144
   Footprints   147
   Bananas in the Boat   157
   Season's End   162

Winter
   Dog Years   167

Afterword
   One Last Walk   170

For the friends and family who have multiplied my joy in the outdoors.

For my dad, who planted the seed for the passions found herein.

For Lucy, the best damn dog I've ever loved.

FOREWORD

Allen Crater is an enigma of sorts. On one hand, he's a certified old soul with a penchant for heirloom leather, vintage wines, and classic hardcover books; on the other, he exudes the youthful, kinetic energy and *joie de vivre* of someone half his age.

"I have to stomp the juice out of the grapes when they're ripe or I get nothing at all," he says. To the envy of onlookers (me, included), he somehow manages to find more free time than the average working stiff — always backpacking, big-game hunting, and fly fishing out West — or anywhere across his native Michigan. He's constantly on the move, a restless spirit more comfortable outdoors than in.

Allen and I first met at the Wealthy Street Theater during

the Fly Fishing Film Tour. He was representing Backcountry Hunters and Anglers, and I was busy signing copies of my latest book, *Flyfisher's Guide to Michigan*. We shared a table and several IPAs while chatting about writing, fishing, and the merits of lucky hats.

By the time the night concluded, I was a card-carrying member of BHA, and Allen left with a copy of *Flyfisher's Guide to Michigan* under his arm. We agreed to stay in touch, but how often are those words uttered in vain? After all, he's a successful business owner, and I spend my days working for The Man. We're both devoted dads and husbands, which makes for the busiest of lives. But somehow, we've managed to find a few hours to hunt, fish, and discuss writing — and my life has been richer as a result.

One of our shared adventures makes an appearance in Allen's essay "Parts Unknown." The fishing had been slow that day — until he tied on a favorite streamer, the infamous black Sex Dungeon. Without giving too much away, let's just say he landed a brown trout that afternoon that would make any angler envious. In print, Allen makes himself sound like a nervous wreck; but in reality, he played that fish with surgical precision.

Outdoor adventures woven together with words — that's what *Outside in Shorts* is all about. As readers, we accompany Allen on trout streams as fog rises from the water; we quiver with excitement in a deer blind on Opening Day; we feel the frustration while searching for a son's lost, lucky hat. Allen even invites us up north to his camp at Shastaland, where we're lulled to sleep by eloquent verse and smooth Irish whisky:

"Swollen raindrops ping on the metal roof of the cabin, like dimes being dropped on the floor, and the steady hiss of the old gas lantern envelopes the small space in its warm light. Soothing. Peaceful. A cool October evening in northern Michigan. My only company is Harrison in hard cover, Jameson in a tin cup, and thoughts of tomorrow's float down one of my favorite rivers with a friend."

In another essay... *"Once again, I feel connected to all things living. The eagle and the trout. The trees and the grass. I gaze into the mysterious water and see myself reflected back. Differently."*

Like Allen the writer, *Outside in Shorts* is a marvelous mystery; a deep, introspective dive into one sportsman's complex relationship with the natural world.

–Jon Osborn
Holland, Michigan

SOLACE IN THE SOLITUDE

When we were kids, my friends and I would make a contest out of who could hold their breath the longest underwater. With all the determination an eight-year-old could muster, I would resist and then physically come to blows with the urge — the panic really — that would set in during these challenges. Head shaking, tiny bubbles slowly escaping. Can't go one second longer... but I would. Maybe even a couple more. And then, just as everything threatened to go dark, a frantic break of the surface, hoping for pride's sake I wasn't the first, taking the air in large desperate gulps, and squinting from the brightness of the day.

January was my gulp of air, the blinding light, the reset button. For five days, I, along with a couple friends, chased through Colorado's wide empty spaces searching for silence,

Solace in the Solitude

solitude, and winter trout.

Geoff, Adam, and I are on I-285 escaping the claustrophobia of the city and the suffocation of the self-induced busyness of the passing season. Like taking off boots at the end of a long day on the trail or removing a hat that fits too tight — the release is welcome and sweet. The traffic, the people, the noise, the ugliness are all fading. No need to jostle. No need to hurry. Just a few friends on the open road, traveling through a flat, empty, and arid landscape. Pink mountains silhouetted on the distant horizon. Our only companions, the occasional groups of pronghorn feeding in the predawn light. Our only music, the rhythmic hum of tires on the road. I can breathe again.

We're catching up with another friend in Buena Vista, where we'll stay in the off-grid cabin he calls his winter home. From there we explore. We wander. We fish. We eat. We drink. We sleep. The cycle repeats. Our agenda is as fluid as the water but finds its own simple rhythm.

Each morning we rise early, the heat from the woodstove chased out hours ago. Despite the lack of snow, it's cold. The thermometer outside reads 11-below. I crawl out of my sleeping bag and climb down the wooden ladder to stoke the fire. The dogs stir from the warmth of their beds. I put on the coffee and get the bacon going, my breath reflected in the glow of my headlamp. We establish our ritual. Coffee. Bacon. Hit the road. Fish until dark. Walk the trails back to the truck by headlamp. Dots, single file in a glowing parade. Hit the local watering hole for dinner, drinks, and sometimes music. Back to the cabin where we gather around the lanterns and the wood stove, sharing stories and nightcaps before finding our way back to our bunks.

We hit the Arkansas, the South Platte, and the Big Thompson and find our winter fish. But, as every angler knows, that's not really what we are looking for. In the wilderness, we discover something far more important. We find solitude and community. Spaces so expansive and so empty our thoughts have room to breathe. A connection that was unwittingly growing faint. And parts of ourselves feared lost. As Abbey famously said, "We need the possibility of escape as surely as we need hope." We found our escape.

Back at the truck we strip off waders and load up. The space empty and silent. The stars bright. The air fresh and cold with a hint of evergreen. I take a long, deep breath and savor it, for soon the contest begins anew.

Spring

A screened window breathes
The season's first, while thunder echoes
In cadence with raindrops pregnant with promise.
The wind carries the scent of wet dirt and budding green.
Birds, again alive, bob and bow in the grass.
I lace up my boots and head to the trail.
It's spring…

FISHING MIRACLES

It was March of 2016, and this time would be different. We'd be on our own.

The previous year, my son, Blake, and I had been invited on a late-spring fishing trip to Ontario, Canada, with one of his football buddies and father. The trip was his birthday present and brought us to a spot brimming with backcountry logging roads and mazes of hidden lakes and rivers. Most importantly, places that held the trophy-sized pike that ice-out in Canada is legendary for.

That outing had been prodigious, and we brought hundreds of fish to the boat, a few well over the 40-inch mark. Before leaving, we laid plans for our return the following year. But, in the meantime, a variety of unfortunate circumstances converged, causing our friends to cancel at the last minute.

I was left with a dilemma — a 13-year-old fishing savant who was about to have his birthday dreams crushed. And, truthfully, I was eager to get back, too. The trouble was that I lacked an appropriate boat and, maybe more so, the confidence to find and then safely navigate the waters that had been virgin ground just last year.

I made a quick call to my dad, who had recently retired, is always up for adventure, and just so happened to have an appropriate vessel. The conversation lasted all of two minutes — he took far less convincing than expected. Now we were committed, and more than a little nervous.

Our eight-hour drive would take us up the heart of lower Michigan, across the Mackinac Bridge, and through Michigan's Upper Peninsula, where we would cross into Canada via the International Bridge in Sault Ste. Marie. From there we had another three hours, following the scenic Trans-Canada Highway (ON-17) over rivers and along Lake Superior to a simple cabin between the towns of Wawa and White River.

The previous year, we used this same cabin as base camp. We'd eat an early breakfast then head out on miles of backcountry roads, boat and motor in the bed of the truck. We'd fish all morning, enjoy a shore lunch – typically freshly caught pike – fish until dark, and then head back to camp for dinner. A perfect system.

But this year, in my infinite wisdom, I added a wrinkle:

Fishing Miracles

camping overnight on one of the more difficult-to-get-to islands from last year's lineup. The plan seemed solid. It would allow more time fishing and ensure we only had to run the water maze once, including shooting the rapids and wrong-turn waterfalls. But this was fairly wild country, loaded with moose, bear, and wolves; so, before we proceeded, I needed agreement on the new plan, which again went easier than anticipated, my crew being either adventurous or gullible.

We left home in the wee hours of the morning, arriving at the first night's cabin by early afternoon. Despite the lack of sleep, we were fully charged with anticipation and began exploring as quickly as possible to make the most of the abbreviated day.

Last year, we'd dubbed one of the smaller remote lakes "Trapper Cabin" for the old, weathered structure sitting high on the southwest shoreline. This productive pool is tucked way back into the wilderness, accessible only through a dizzying spider web of two-tracks, which lead to smaller two-tracks, which lead to what can be best described as fold-in-the-mirrors trails, and then a long haul down to the lake. We elected to leave the watercraft behind. I wasn't even sure I could find the damn place, but I *was* sure I didn't want to try while dragging a trailer behind. And I certainly didn't want to try to carry the boat down to the lake with my aging body supported by my 13-year-old son and recently retired father.

We were able to locate the lake. Okay, that's not entirely

accurate. My son, who can't remember to put on deodorant without being reminded, was somehow able to navigate us through backcountry roads, two-tracks, and switchbacks directly to this tiny hidden kettle-pond that he had been to exactly one time before, miles from anything vaguely resembling civilization. By memory. I was dumbfounded. Happy, but truly and utterly dumbfounded. It was a fishing miracle. One of several we would encounter on this trip.

We grabbed our gear and began exploring on foot. And that was when I began to realize how grossly I had underestimated the true ruggedness of the Canadian landscape. We trudged through wetlands and tangles of densely packed cedars; over hills; and through thickets of face-scratching, clothes-tearing prickers, dodging the droppings of both moose and bear until we *finally* reached a point on the lake that offered meager access to cast from shore. We were hot, sweaty, scratched, tired, bug bitten, and grinning from ear to ear.

Junior's second cast with a Johnson Silver Minnow had him hooked up with a decent northern that he managed to wrangle to shore and quickly release amidst violent headshakes. This is what we had come for. To a man, we Craters are a competitive lot, especially when fishing is involved. After the boy landed his fifth or sixth fish, the trash talk began, and I started to wonder if my previous year's success was truly a case of beginner's luck. I could foresee the rest of my trip filled with moments where I was out-navigated, out-fished, and, in no uncertain terms, out-bragged by this grinning boy whose neck I desperately wanted to wring at the moment.

Eventually we *all* got into some good fish, delaying, for the time being, any need for violence.

After catching enough to placate ourselves, we wound around the tangled shoreline, back through the logging-road maze, and to the cabin for a warm dinner and a heated game of Yahtzee.

The next morning, in the dim pre-dawn hours, we loaded the boat with fishing gear, the cooler, three-man tent, a pack filled with clothes and sleeping bags, a water filter, and a small backpacking camp stove. We were heading out to find my island, and the small boat was loaded to the gills.

This part was going to be a little tricky. We had to navigate across a large, desolate lake and through a minefield of underwater rocks that rise up unexpectedly from the deep — the demise of at least one outboard motor on the last trip. From there we'd wind our way through a maze of outlets and connecting rivers, up and over an eight-to-ten-foot rapid, through a shallow channel, and into another lake deep inside the Canadian backcountry. Once in the upper lake, we had to make our way to the other end where we would find our island paradise and do most of our fishing.

Armed with an old GPS, a poor map, and last year's fuzzy memory, we slowly traversed the labyrinth in our overloaded and underpowered boat only to arrive at a spot that neither my son nor I recognized. The lake appeared to simply end. My instincts insisted we needed to stay right, but my 13-year-old, who had successfully navigated us to "Trapper Cabin," thought we needed to go left. My dad, who had never been there before, simply smiled and shrugged. All eyes were on me to make the call, and I felt the weight of the decision heavier than before. Wrong turns on this stretch of water lead to waterfalls, and the safety of my dad and son and the success or failure of this trip rested on my choice. We eased into the bay, and then suddenly, a previously hidden route revealed itself. Yep, this was it.

We entered the river portion of the journey and began to navigate upstream against the current, dodging rocks, beaver dams, and gravel bars that seemed more common than last season. And then we came to a whirlpool lying just below an intimidating froth of rapids. Last year, we were able to gun it upstream and hang on. This year, water levels were much lower, exposing formidable rocks and ensuring that a boat loaded with three guys and gear and powered by a meager 15-horse motor was not going to make it.

Completely discouraged and with no real Plan B, we motored over to a peninsula that looked to have an old portage route designed for canoe travel. The uphill trail was relatively short but littered with large rocks and tree limbs. It was debatable whether we could wrangle our aluminum vessel up the treacherous path, but I was determined to try. This was the highlight of our trip after all, and the only way to the tremendous fishing that lay beyond.

We unloaded all the gear but soon realized that the outboard motor was securely padlocked to the boat and the keys lay many miles away, back in the truck. We would have to carry the boat with the motor attached, another obstacle that made success even less likely. But then, by some act of providence, a boat full of anglers who appeared to be locals motored up slowly behind us. Clearly bemused at our situation, they got out and we began to talk. A "block M" hat worn by one of the crew was my first indication that these guys might be okay. Turned out that they were from Michigan and were staying in a cabin not far away — an annual tradition. Better yet, they had a roller system packed with them specifically for this occasion. In a way common among folks from the Mitten State, these guys rolled up their sleeves; laid the track; and helped us push, pull, shove, swear, lift, carry, and drag our boat up to the lake. We, of course, promptly returned the favor. That was the last we saw of them. Another fishing miracle.

After reloading, we made our way slowly across the upper lake, more conscious than ever of the below-average water levels and not wishing to tempt fate further. Soon the island came into sight. We pulled up and hopped out to inspect what I hoped would be our home for the night. A clear flat area with tremendous views and an old fire ring offered evidence that this spot would work perfectly. Fresh moose scat indicated that we were not the only creatures to inhabit this small sanctuary, even if only briefly. We unloaded all the camping gear, set up the tent, and motored off to get after some fish. This location had been very productive last year, and I was eager to prove to my dad that coming along had been a good decision.

We began working water that had previously delivered fish after fish, but the action was slow. The look on my son's face betrayed the sinking feeling that was beginning to overtake me. There were fish here, and big ones at that. But, finding them would be the challenge.

We slowly began to unravel the mystery of the water — a few small ones hitting and then more, with some larger specimens mixed in. It ended up being a pretty good day. An amazing day, really, by any measure other than the success we had the previous year. We made our way back to camp, started a fire, and got water boiling for dinner courtesy of Mountain House. The appetizer would be beef stroganoff followed by the main course of chicken teriyaki with rice. Bodies sore but bellies full and warmed by the fire, we watched the sun dip slowly over the horizon as the sky turned from yellow to blazing orange and then a deep red before winking out, leaving only speckled stars and the mournful call of the loons. We slept well that night, dreaming of the fish the next day would bring, the challenges now a long-forgotten memory. Yet again, another fishing miracle.

After a quick camp breakfast, we were back out and working the water that produced the day before. Again, we found fish, but not nearly like last year. We decided to move into the shallows, and our success rate increased exponentially. The telltale wake of a predator just before the strike is more potent than the strongest morning coffee. Fuel to press on.

We fished hard in the shifting winds until well after lunch, surviving on a few sparse snacks, before finally deciding to test a small downwind cove. The first cast produced a quick strike. Nothing big. Reeling in though, I realized that this fish might be larger than anticipated. Leaning hard on the rod, I steered him toward the side and finally caught a glimpse. He was an absolute monster — measuring upwards of 50 inches. My son fumbled for the net and then suddenly, in a concussive splash, the fish was gone. But wait, maybe not. Something was still fighting on the end of my line. I reeled in only to find a hammer-handle bleeding from giant teeth marks and deep wounds down his side. Damn. We speculated that he was attacked by the larger fish who spooked and released near the bow. We had found the big boys.

Dad struggled to navigate us into the cove and maintain our casting position while fighting the rising wind. A consecutive cast resulted in a strong hit almost immediately after touching the water, and I landed a solid 30-incher. Blake fired a cast and hooked up with another large fish. During the retrieve, it raced directly under the boat before breaking off. In the meantime, I began casting again. As my lure neared the side on the retrieve, a giant mouth completely enveloped the Johnson Silver

Minnow. I screamed. Loud. And then began giggling. Like a little girl. This was a really good fish, and he was running. I fought to bring him alongside while my son scrambled for the net. He was able to make the scoop and fought to lift the trophy into the boat. It was a beautiful northern that went forty-plus. We were ecstatic. Next cast, another hook-up. And then one for Junior. Another breakoff. Another monster to the boat. And so it went for about the next half hour. Giant fish after giant fish. I willed this moment to last forever — the fishing, the time with my father and son. I tried to hold it, like water in my hand. But the sun was moving down the horizon, the wind was picking up, and we still needed to get back to the island, pack up, fight the wind across the lake, portage the boat and gear, run the maze, navigate the rocks, and take the boat out — preferably not in the dark.

One last cast turned into a couple until we reluctantly left the best fishing any of us had ever experienced. Smiles on our faces, adrenaline coursing our veins, and wind whipping in our faces, we made our way back as waves broke over the gunwale and the sun slipped below the horizon. I took one quick glance back and gave silent thanks for fishing miracles, knowing this magic half-hour would live on in stories shared around campfires and memories that grow only sweeter with age.

THE PRESERVATION OF FIRE

It snowed last night. Just a light dusting, but enough to turn things white again. We throw in another log and stoke the wood stove to warm frozen boots errantly left outdoors.

Mesmerized by the red and amber flames dancing just behind the glass, I'm reminded of a quote from Gustav Mahler that my friend, Jon Osborn, is fond of: "Tradition is not the worship of ashes, but the preservation of fire."

It's my first true "trout camp." I've never really paid much attention to the trout opener, typically fishing year-round on my home waters, but I was excited when the invite came. A small gathering at a buddy's northern Michigan cabin. Like deer camp, it's more about the camaraderie than anything else. The fishing is just a bonus, or perhaps an excuse to spend time with others who share my passions, provide different viewpoints, and know when to call bullshit on my tall tales — not that it keeps me from sharing them.

It's a place of daily rituals.

Breakfast together in the cabin as the sun rises over the dark water, both pots brewing to keep up. To the gravel launch as we begin the day's float. Moving quietly along, the sounds of the awakening forest provide the underscore.

Lunch, a harvest from the previous season, cooked over flame, while soaking up the peace of the moment, sun on our faces. Floating on as a few bugs begin to show themselves. Trout gently nosing the surface, creating rings that radiate out like time itself. Bent rods following splashy takes. Satisfied releases offered back in gratitude to the cold river.

Dinner together around the table as daylight fades; swapping stories, ribbing over the fish I missed because of a bad knot, and reliving the highlights, fish by fish, bend by bend. Maybe a cocktail or two and a pipe around the pop-and-crackle of the stove as the moon climbs higher. Tall tales get taller and traditions take root.

Off to bed. Dreams of tomorrow's jeweled trout fresh in mind. Attempting sleep despite the poorly tuned, chainsaw-like sounds rising and falling from the other side of the room, verifying last call came one drink too late.

On the river we find the current slowly pulling us into the future while crossing paths with a few others carrying out traditions from years gone by. Some of the camps getting smaller now as age and illness and other life responsibilities thin the ranks, the hardy few carrying on to pass the flame.

We hear stories of those no longer with us, trout from back when "the fishing was better," snow so deep the trucks got stuck, camp mishaps, pranks, drinks, awards, and rituals. You can feel it. The fire still burns. Preserved in the sharing, at least for one season more.

These days, my fishing isn't about the heft of the stringer, it's about making the most of the unknown handful of moments I've been allotted. Of spending the ever-dwindling sand in my hourglass in a meaningful way. Among people I care about and places that leave an imprint.

I recently read a quote that stuck with me, though I do not know who penned it. "No matter the risks we take, we always consider the end to be too soon, even though in life, more than anything else, quality should be more important than quantity." At 48, this struck home. The end does, already, seem too soon. But my fire still burns. And moments like these, spent on the water with friends, provide both the tinder and the seasoned logs I need.

Ayn Rand famously said: "Do not let your fire go out, spark by irreplaceable spark in the hopeless swamps of the not-quite, the not-yet, and the not-at-all. Do not let the hero in your soul perish in lonely frustration…" And I, for one, do not intend to.

Can't Be Done

I distinctly remember flying around the old logging road corner watching the boat trailer roll up hard on one wheel. Way up. Positive it was going over and pissed about smacking my head on the ceiling of the Jeep and spilling my beer. Our gear was everywhere, mixed with old McDonald's bags, tins of Kodiak, dog toys, and empties. You just laughed, and, by some miracle, the trailer righted itself in a haze of dust. And then we fished.

And that is who you were. Fearless, with your foot to the mat. Always on the slimmest edge. Bigger than any moment or any room. Life-volume set to eleven, all the time.

And that, perhaps, is what made our friendship so unique. Me the uptight one with schedules and plans, always needing

Can't Be Done

to be prepared; you, with no schedule and no plan, always taking the moments as they came.

Like that time we planned to get in a quick after-work river session. I was, of course, there and ready at the prescribed time, gear organized, rod lined, fly selected, and wadered-up. Waiting on you. Thinking maybe you'd forgotten. But, fifteen minutes late, you rolled in, out of the car before it even slammed to a stop. Soon after, realizing you'd forgotten not only your flies, but more importantly your waders. I figured we'd just call it, but you saw no issue wet-wading in boxers and dress shoes. And hell, I had plenty of flies for both of us, right?

Damn, we fished a lot.

I still remember the invitation to join you and your buddies on the Holy Waters of the Au Sable during your annual trip. My first time. Rolling in, fly rod with no leader or tippet, a couple random flies from the local shop, my waders and boots still in the boxes that arrived on my doorstep the day before. And the requisite casserole for dinner one night. To say I was a little green would be like saying the sun is slightly hot. I walked in the cabin only to find you all sleeping off the adventures from the night before, so I put some coffee on and waited on the deck. Then those guys went upriver to huck streamers while you helped me get lined up and we worked our way downstream. You patiently instructing. Me a messy student. I'll never forget that first fish, an eight-inch planter that is still my greatest trophy.

Then later that night, after steaks on the grill and way more than the twelver I ridiculously brought along, a game of Yahtzee. Me infuriated that you would take four threes for your "four of a kind" when you clearly needed them to get your bonus on top. You, maybe not in the clearest state of mind, but confident in your plan yelling, "Don't micromanage my Yahtzee game." A phrase I still use. A meaning only I really know.

After that, we fished together as often as possible. The Pere Maquette, the Jordan, the Rogue, the Muskegon, the Flat. Whenever we could for whatever was biting. From blazing hot summer nights searching for smallies, to subzero winter mornings chasing chrome.

I remember that rising trout tucked into the timber with a weird current that you tried over and over and over to catch until finally relenting saying, "Can't be done." Another Matt-ism I sometimes use.

I remember slamming through a sweeper and nearly taking you out of the boat the first time I ran the sticks. I remember chugging Hot Damn because I couldn't stop shaking after catching that huge brown mousing together. I remember you on the net, slippery gravel and filled waders. I remember days in the boat so cold our beer froze, and playing pull tabs at Na-Tah-Ka waiting for our feet to thaw. I remember you tying on a rusty Mepps you found on the bank out of desperation on that slow night on the Rogue. I remember being chased out of the river by lightning, satisfied to drink soggy beers on the tailgate and watch the storm roll through. And I remember your wedding reception and those trout-shaped bottle openers you and Laurie gave out. I still carry mine.

I remember arguing and bullshitting and laughing. Lots of fucking laughing.

I remember you challenging me to write down my life goals, or at least guideposts, which I did:

First, Choose Adventure. *Intentionally choose opportunities for adventure and when life offers multiple paths, choose the most adventurous.*

Second, Invest in Relationships That Matter. *Spend your time, energy, emotion, and money on the relationships in your life that matter and spend heavily.*

Last, Grow Every Day. *Find ways to improve mentally, physically, and emotionally every day.*

Honestly, Matt, I've tried to live them. But I don't always get it right. Hell, I get it wrong more than not. You were always trying to get me to loosen up, and I was always trying to get you to button down.

I remember that last time on the river together, fishing the Hex. What a debacle. That was the night I decided I wasn't cut out to do life on eleven and stopped answering the invites.

I remember you calling out of the blue last summer, wanting to get together with the families and my bullshit excuse to dodge it. I remember the Christmas card you sent this year with you and Laurie and the kids.

And I remember getting the call from Pasco this past Friday, letting me know you had passed. Just like that. Well before your time. And sitting in shock. The guilt choked up in my throat. Trying to stop the tears from staining my face when I tried to swallow it. Then thinking to myself, "*Can't be done,*" and letting them flow like a steady current. Ashamed and embarrassed.

I miss your laughter already. And the arguments. And the push to live more fully, that seems even more relevant today.

THE RIVER GIVES

It's May in Michigan. The season has been wet with weather that can't quite make up its mind. A few days ago the furnace was running, today the temps will hit 90. We're playing a guessing game at this point. The hatches are sporadic, the rain comes in deluges, and the rivers are running high and dirty. But make no mistake, we will be fishing.

There's a famous quote by Michigan native, John Voelker (Robert Traver) that, while highly overused, still remains incredibly poignant: *"I fish because I love to; because I love the environs where trout are found, which are invariably beautiful, and hate the environs where crowds of people are found, which are invariable ugly; because of the television commercials, cocktail parties and assorted social posturing I thus escape; because, in a world where* most men seem to spend their lives doing things they hate, my fishing is at once an endless source of delight and an act of small rebellion; because trout do not lie or cheat but respond only to quietude and humility and endless patience; because I suspect that men are going along this way for the last time, and I for one don't want to waste the trip; because mercifully there are no telephones on trout waters; because only in the woods can I find solitude without loneliness; because bourbon out of an old tin cup tastes better out there; because maybe someday I will catch a mermaid; and, finally, not because I regard fishing as being so terribly important but because I suspect that so many of the other concerns of men are equally unimportant – and not nearly so much fun."

Reading these words, I can't help but wonder if Voelker was envisioning this very spot when he penned them. Certainly I go fishing to catch fish, but it's so much more than that. I go to let my worries wash downstream like so much sediment after a hard rain; to listen to the quiet of nature and hear my own thoughts more clearly; for the solitude that can still be gained among friends who understand; to smell the cedar-tinged newness of a spring morning or the damp humid close to a night in the summer; because the river is alluring and mysterious and occasionally gives up her secrets to those patient enough. Henry David Thoreau said it this way: "*Many men go fishing all of their lives without knowing that it is not fish they are after.*" Thankfully, at my age, I do know.

Like Voelker, I, too, suspect we are going along this way

The River Gives

for the last time, and I don't want to waste the trip either. I'm with a few close friends as evening begins to close on the nearly deserted river tucked deep in the forested byways we call "Up North." Our spirited conversations accented by the chorus of peepers, the call of an oriole, the splash of a beaver's tail, and the occasional quiet sip of a trout.

The fishing is slow, but we don't mind. Our rhythms have slowed in turn, punctuated by the occasional burst of adrenaline fueled by the take of a trout. Over the course of the float, we've coalesced with the river. Become immersed in her beauty and soothed by her voice. We've felt her pull. And while she has been slow to give up the fish, somehow, she always knows what we need and provides.

It's May in Michigan, and tonight the river gives.

A Day on the Water

Rubber drones on concrete as we drive in silence, still at odds over the music selection. I'm with my oldest son, home for the summer from school in Bozeman. He's feeling a little country. I'm feeling a little rock and roll.

We're on our way to pick up his college roommate, another Michigander drawn west. Finally settling on what could best be described as Southern rock, we each take solace in a perceived victory.

Today will be my first chance to fish or spend any real time with him at all since his coming home. He's been busy, working twelve-hour days with bills to pay. But this is our time. The raft is loaded, the cooler is full, and the schedule is cleared.

A Day on the Water

Collin is already waiting, and we're quickly back on the road. I'm quiet, listening to them share college stories. These two have grown close over this year in school and fish together any time they have a break in homework — although I secretly suspect a few classes have been sacrificed in the name of trout. I keep my thoughts to myself and let them carry on.

The bank to the river is steep. Hazy clouds disperse the morning sun, keeping the air cool and comfortable. Small sippers dot the surface, and a handful of caddis bounce along the water in a ritual as old as time. Satisfied, we carry the raft down and finish loading gear.

I take first shift on the oars, feathering them in the heavy current while the boys, eager for first fish, cast to the small risers. No dice, but miles of water still lay ahead. The oars find their rhythm as we meld with the current, picking out fish as we go. A few other boats have claimed this stretch, so we quickly fish our way through, eager to find clean water.

Warmed by the sun and the coffee, I peel off a layer and pull with intention across the big water. We have this section to ourselves, save for one other well-used drift boat with a solo passenger. He doesn't seem to be fishing but rather watching us, until finally he moves downstream to the next run. We fish and drift down as he slides to the inside.

He gives a quick wave, and I nod back. There's something on his mind; he rows close. "White with a little brown has been hot." He tosses a couple flies into our raft and quietly floats on.

It's time to make a switch, and Collin takes over in the middle seat while I move to the front. I pull out the eight-weight, rig up with twelve-pound mono, and tie on one of the new streamers. A test in the water meets with unanimous approval.

Working down, we find a new run with a fast inside seam and a little back eddy that looks fishy. I manage a long cast into the dark water and give a little twitch. Before I can even start stripping there's a flash; my line goes tight. I know immediately that this is a good fish. Everything else in the boat stops.

He's running now but hooked well. There's a nervous energy. I try to muscle him toward the boat, but he's not ready, peeling off more line as he surges for the heavy current. "Let him run," Kyle anxiously implores. But I'm back on the reel as Collin grabs the net. I work him closer, but he's running again and starting to tire. I finally work him close enough for the scoop. He's strong to the end, but the line holds.

The net hangs heavy in the water alongside the boat. I'm shaking but shrug off the excitement, my voice betraying me a little. The fishermen guessing begins in earnest. "He's at least twenty, maybe twenty-two." We celebrate and snap a few quick pictures before sending him back. He swims off slowly, in that sullen way bigger fish often do. I need a minute.

Back to the middle seat while the boys continue to fish, and we each make the expected comments about quality over quantity. The setting sun brings out more bugs. We take our

A Day on the Water

time, waiting on a spinner fall that never materializes but secretly know we just aren't ready for the day to end.

There's a lightness to the moment, but the undertones are weighty. The river. My son. The fish. The kindness of a stranger. The silence and the steady flow of the water moving ever forward, like our short time together. A noticeable coolness returns to the air, and I shiver on the way to the take-out.

THE BEST WATER STILL LIES AHEAD

The tartar-sauce-smeared walleye sandwich, deep-fried tater tots, and tall Two Hearted hit all the right notes — more than can be said for the guy wearing the Hawaiian shirt and belting out '80s covers from the back corner of the bar.

It's the Friday before Michigan's trout opener, and I'm in Dingman's with my buddy Koz; the place is packed. A dusty gravel parking lot crammed with jacked-up diesels, tricked-out trail-ready Wranglers, and more than a few side-by-sides tells you everything you need to know about our fellow patrons.

A low cheer rises in the room, and we both nod our agreement that Seattle got a steal grabbing MSU's Kenneth Walker with the 41st pick. I take another sip of beer and smirk at Koz as the gentleman from table four takes his best shot with

The Best Water Still Lies Ahead

the slender, slightly tatted bartender sporting painted-on jeans and a low-cut t-shirt. The salvo falls safely short, embarrassingly evident to everyone but him. She flashes a practiced smile and wiggles past. Chalk up another big tip to courage in a can and a healthy side of pre-season bravado. On a night like tonight, it's easy to feel a little swagger, warranted or not.

After dinner, we opt for the backroad route to Koz's place and swing through the campground upriver to size up the competition. It's about what we expected. A cacophony of trailers, tents, tarps, and even an impressive totem-turned-flagpole form the small symphony of opening-day optimists. We roll past with a polite wave.

Back at the cabin, Jason pulls in just in front of us. He grabs his gear, and we all head inside to get out of the chill, each staking out our respective bunk before pouring a few drinks, finding a cozy chair, and laying plans around the radiant-orange wood stove.

The forecast looks encouraging, a relative metric here in the Great Lakes state. The weatherman on 9-and-10 News tells us tomorrow will be warmish with in-and-out sun followed by a good rain overnight. The fact that he delivers it with a straight face is convincing enough, and, like Lion's fans on draft night, a "this-is-our-year" glow suddenly fills the cabin. With a low-pressure system moving in and temps that could touch 60, we are hopeful for Hennies and chart our course accordingly.

Foolproof plan in place, we all but high-five ourselves while mentally snapping grip-n-grins and carefully returning golden trophies back to silver streams. Bend by bend we work the water in our conversations, at some point losing count of all the fish we've brought to hand, the excitement rising in climatic crescendo. Warmed by the fire, assured success, and the contents of a charred-oak barrel, we finally turn in, chasing a sunrise that can't come soon enough.

Like an eight-year-old on Christmas Eve, shut-eye proves elusive, my anticipation barely dulled by the liberal doses of rocks-glass sleep medicine I've consumed. I toss and turn, playing the events of tomorrow's float over and over in my mind's eye, and walking through my fly selection one final time. The click-click of the wall clock offers a tortured testament to time traveling too slow.

Darkness. The coffee begins its pre-programmed brew, and moments later, the rich aroma of the pot's contents hits, coaxing me awake. Mustering all of my concentration, I manage to pry one eye open and then the next. Rubbing the blur away, I'm bid good-morning by a wash of pinkish-purple sky over the dark river just out the front pane. A good omen to be sure.

The birds are starting to get rowdy in that first-light-of-day kind of way, and there's quiet stirring in the cabin. Untangling myself from the sleeping bag, I tug on some sweatpants, pull on my lucky hat, and stumble to the bathroom before grabbing some coffee and heading outside to have a smoke. The morning has "*that feeling*" to it. Like porn, it's hard to describe but you know it when you see it.

On the deck, I sip the first of the black elixir and finish my cigarette, watching the tannic water slide slowly past. A breeze as faint as a whisper tickles the trees. For a brief time, I'm lost in the rhythm of the river and only dragged back into the present by the wafting scent of breakfast. Koz is a wizard in the kitchen, and soon we are stuffed to the point of discomfort.

We clean up and start gathering gear, still waiting on two more friends that will join us for the eight-hour float. Kevin is a podiatrist from Traverse City, and Sam is a water-quality biologist for the local tribe.

They roll in just before 8:30, excited. We quickly wader up and head out, wanting to be first down this stretch of water. The air has the slightly damp fresh-dirt smell best described as "spring anticipation," and marsh marigolds pepper the swampy drive.

German legend tells of the first marsh marigold. A young maiden named Caltha (meaning "cup" in Greek) fell so in love with the sun god that she spent her days and nights in the fields, trying to see as much of him as possible, until her body and spirit slowly wasted away. The first marsh marigold — a cup filled with the sun's rays — grew where the devoted maiden had stood.

Spring is the undisputed season of optimism, and the maiden's message is not lost on us.

Finally at the parking area, we wrangle the boats down the wooden launch and catch up with a couple other buddies who stop by — planning to start at the next put-in upstream. It's agreed that today is the day; there's something you can just feel in the air. We bid them good luck and promise to leave a few untouched fish.

There may not be a moment filled with greater expectancy than when creaky oars first break water on the trout opener. We jostle for position out front, and Jason and I manage to win the duel, with Koz, Sam, and Kevin just behind. I start in the bow, rigged with a streamer, knowing we'll be hitting the better hatch water later when the day warms up. We'll switch spots after each fish, rotating between bow and sticks. A quick "yeee-haw," and we're off.

The first few casts are sloppy, as always, before I finally tamp down the adrenaline and shake off the pre-game jitters. In a rhythm now, every shot providing the puckered anticipation of a strike. I hit each pocket, testing the bank and thick timber while Jason deftly maneuvers us into position. Nothing yet, but any moment will bring the season's first, and then we can all breathe again.

An hour or so in and we've yet to move a fish. I'm not alarmed. We are, after all, barely into the first quarter, and the better water is down around the next bend or two anyway. But still, a small morsel of doubt is planted. We make the corner, and the wind noticeably picks up. I shoot a glance at Jason; we both know that behind the wind and around this bend lies our opportunity.

Another hour passes. It's a little premature, but I'm anxious and switch flies again, this time going straight to the "can't miss" black Sex Dungeon that I probably should have started with in the first place. "Dark day, dark fly," they say, and the building cloud cover affirms the inevitable. No more messing around.

The weather shift and my favorite fly have me feeling confident, but, in fishing, there's a fine line between optimism and insanity. After another half hour or so of fruitless flogging I'm spent like a mayfly spinner and reluctantly slip into the middle seat while Jason hops up front to close the deal.

Two hours later, we decide it's time to stop for lunch. A mid-day rally is desperately needed, and brats on the grill chased down with carbonated hops are just the fuel we need. The air carries a hint of humidity, and we make quick work of the eating so we can get back to the fishing. The water on the last half of the float is a veritable bug factory, and the weather signals an imminent hatch. I take one last drag, extinguish the cigarette, and we shove off, eyes glued to the river for telltale rings and stealthy sips.

It starts slowly, first a few small BWOs, then a few bigger ones, and finally a Hendrickson here and there. A faint rise, and another. Nothing consistent, but enough to make us pay attention. It's all *finally* starting to unfold. We float a few parachute patterns down the bubble line but find no takers. I switch up, electing a modified Klinkhammer emerger specially tied by my buddy Ozzy for this very moment. I make the drift, go untouched, and exhale the breath I was holding in. Everything is unnaturally quiet. The talking has stopped, each intently focused as we present our offerings.

And then a heavy splat hits the brim of my hat and another finds my hand. The air has grown thick, and the wind feels like it's about to make a switch. *Splat.* Another drop hits my sleeve. And then the breeze brushes the back of my neck, cooler now. The splats become more regular, pinging off the cooler and sides of the boat. I pull on my rain jacket and look up. The sky is ominous, and the hatch has completely shut down.

I turn to Jason. "Looks like we are back to streamer weather." He nods his agreement, and I switch rods as he pulls anchor. Luckily, the section just below the next bridge is prime streamer water, having proven itself several times in the past.

Koz's boat moves to the front, and we push through some of the less-desirable spots as the rain intensifies. Under the bridge we follow the current on the left and slide into position to fish the channel just upstream from our friends. We work all the way through the tail-out without so much as a follow and finally decide to move on. Pushing through a slower shallow stretch, we come to the whirlpool. The crew in front has hopped out to thoroughly cover it, so we glide past and focus on the deep undercut clay bank on the right. But I'm simply going through the motions at this point.

The Best Water Still Lies Ahead

We're still a solid hour and a half from our take-out and soaking wet. I offer to switch up with Jason, but he declines, and we keep moving down, barely slowing to fish. I make a few half-hearted attempts at anything that looks especially juicy, but I'm tired and getting cold. Pride assures that neither of us will be the one to call it; but at this point, we are just pushing through and we both know it, collectively lured by thoughts of a warm fire and fresh drink waiting at the end.

Back at the cabin, we tie up the boats and unload in the rain. Kevin and Sam have to take off, so we say our good-byes and our "we'll get 'em next times" and watch as they roll out. Back inside we change into dry clothes, and I immediately get to work on a fire while Jason pours cocktails and Koz gets the charcoal going and preps the steaks. Nothing soothes a tough day like red meat on a grill and bourbon in a glass.

After dinner, I sneak out under the back porch to burn one last cigarette before settling into a comfy seat with my comfy drink. Warmed by the fire and the spirits, we begin planning tomorrow's float while wet pellets ping on the metal roof. We tune in the local news and the weatherman says tomorrow will be little warmer with heavy cloud cover and a slight chance of rain. A perfect streamer day.

Eventually, the fire burns down, the glasses dry up, and the lights go out. Back in the bunk, I close my eyes to the *click-click* of the wall clock, waiting on morning, knowing the best water still lies ahead.

Summer

A small campfire crackles.
Drifting asleep to the lap of waves
And the faint chirp of crickets in the thick air.
The lake is warm and smells of fish and seaweed.
But steam rises in the cool morning sunrise.
I grab my rod and head for the river.
It's summer…

The Last Frontier

The sound of a calving glacier is difficult to describe. It starts with a loud crack, like the hands of an angry god clapping, but quickly becomes a low rumble that you feel more than hear. It's a sensation that seems to unfold in slow motion. Like an echo. It's haunting. Powerful. It makes you realize how insignificant you really are.

It was only our second day in Alaska, and it was already earning its reputation as one of the most wild and beautiful places on earth. Leaving Resurrection Bay in Seward, my wife, two teenaged sons, and I were on a boat tour of the Kenai Fjords National Park, which covers an incomprehensible 587,000 acres. The calving of the thirty-story Aialik Glacier was the icing on the cake. That morning we had already witnessed orcas breech and swim under our boat; humpbacks rise, spout, and disappear; sea lions sunning themselves on island rocks; otters playing for the crowd; and black bears foraging along the steep cliffs of the offshore islands — all the while surrounded by mountains capped in whites and blues and more glaciers than we could count. It was easy to get lulled into the idea that this was all part of some carefully choreographed show — until the cold wind rushed down over the glacier, followed by a loud crack, and the hair standing up on the back of your neck assured you that this was, indeed, real, raw, and very powerful.

Our trip was over a year in the making and now finally a reality. Alaska is so expansive and, in many areas, inaccessible, that surveying it thoroughly would take the better part of a lifetime. With just ten days, we were only able to hit a small sampling for our highlight reel. We would fly into Anchorage, rent an SUV, and then travel down the Kenai Peninsula to Seward. After two days of exploring, we would make our way farther south to Homer for two more days, then journey up through Cooper Landing and on to Palmer for two days of recovery before pushing up to Talkeetna and through to Denali for the final three days. Along the way, we would hike, fish, raft, eat, drink, and soak up as much of the wildlife and jaw-dropping mountain views as possible.

The scenic village of Seward is located at the terminus of both the Alaska Railroad and the Seward Highway. Flanked by rugged mountains on one side and the sparkling Resurrection Bay on the other, this charming town of 2,700 is one-hundred percent Alaska. On our last night, we sat out by the fire at our cabin, listening to the meandering stream, interrupted only by the splashing of a salmon making its final journey.

From Seward, we made our way west toward the coast of the Cook Inlet before bearing south to the city of Homer. Affectionately known as the "Cosmic Hamlet by the Sea," Homer is one part fishing town and one part hippie enclave; the Halibut Capital of the World and the end of the road for people who just want to set up shop in a VW bus and go off the grid. It has a vibrant art scene, bustling docks, cloudy mountains jutting straight out of the ocean, and broken-down buses (and boats) reconstructed by those with vagabond hearts. An article published by *The Seattle Times* quoted that Homer is, "a sort of Key West in a parka" — and that may come the closest to anything else I've heard.

We wandered Homer's desolate beaches, explored the local art scene and, of course, tried our hand at some fishing. Our halibut charter included a tranquil two-hour ride, followed by intense fishing for another two before making the trip back.

Chasing these fish was different than any type of angling I had done before. Halibut feed near the bottom, and we were fishing in 170 feet of water. The rods are short and very stout and use three-pound weights to sink the bait, attached to very large hooks, to the bottom. From there, it's three cranks up to wait for a strike, which typically happens within thirty seconds or so. Then, the arm-burning retrieve begins as you retrieve both the fish, which run in the twelve to twenty-five-pound range, plus the weighted sinker, from 170 feet of water. It's work, but loads of fun and some of the best-tasting seafood anywhere in the world. We took some of our catch to Pattie's, out on the spit, where they prepared it fresh for us while we watched eagles tussle over their dinner on the beach.

The next morning, we rose early, slated for a long travel day up to Palmer, broken up by a half-day fly-fishing float on the Kenai River out of Cooper Landing. Cooper Landing (population 289) is located at the confluence of Kenai Lake and the Kenai River and immediately felt like a place I could call home, with its beautiful aquamarine rivers, rising slopes, and laid-back mountain-town vibe. It was first settled in the 19th century by gold and mineral prospectors and has since become a popular summer destination thanks to its scenic wilderness location and proximity to a world-class salmon fishery. But we weren't here for the salmon; our sights were set on wild rainbows and dolly varden. Though we were a little early in the season for the gigantic trout that follow the salmon spawn and have made this upper section of river famous, our guide put us on some great fish and we brought eighteen of them to hand in our four-hour float. We grabbed brisket and beverages at Sackett's Kenai Grill, a local favorite, and hit the road again.

Palmer lies on the north shore of the Matanuska River not

far above tidewater, in a wide valley between the Talkeetna Mountains to the north and the Chugach Mountains to the south and east. It's a beautiful little town and the last real "city" before Denali. We rolled in under heavy cloud cover and a light, misting rain.

From Palmer, Hatcher Pass took us to Talkeetna and Denali. Hatcher is a beautiful and rugged twenty-two-mile gravel mountain pass through the southwest part of the Talkeetna Mountains. It is named after Robert Hatcher, a prospector and miner. It divides the alpine headwaters of Willow Creek on the west from Fishhook Creek and the Independence Bowl on the east side. To the east, the road drops and follows the Little Susitna River canyon downstream, and south, some dozen miles to the abrupt mountain front at the edge of the broad Mananuska-Susitna Valley.

Once through the pass, it was on to Talkeetna, which sits at the convergence of three glacier-fed rivers: the Susitna, Chulitna, and Talkeetna. Talkeetna began in 1916, when the area was chosen as a district headquarters for the Alaska Railroad. The core downtown area is classified as a National Historic Site with buildings dating from the early 1900s, including Nagley's General Store, Fairview Inn, and the Talkeetna Roadhouse. Talkeetna is the base for expeditions to Denali and plays the part of old mountain town perfectly. Tourists travel to here to fish, raft, mountain bike, camp, hunt, and go flightseeing. On clear days, some of the best views of

Denali and the Alaska Range can be seen right from the end of Main Street. The town is an eclectic mix of railroad workers, bush pilots, guides, oarsman, and tourists from all over the world. We soaked in its charm, hit up the Roadhouse for their famous cinnamon rolls, and grabbed lunch and beer (root beer for the boys) at Denali Brewing before getting back on the road.

For our time in Denali, we had rented a cabin in the town of Healy, just outside the National Park and Preserve. The cabin owner, Mike, it turned out, was a Michigan native, hailing from Grayling (population 1,900) who moved to Alaska to escape the "crowds" and traffic. Like most Alaskans, Mike was a generous host with the kind of inner resilience required to call this place home. Mike's father was a famous builder of Au Sable River boats — unique vessels found only in Grayling, Michigan, that have been used on the Au Sable and Manistee river systems for the last hundred and thirty years. With this connection, both geographically and through the addiction known as fly-fishing, Mike and I had a lot to talk about, until I finally relented so he could get back to an endless list of chores.

For our first day, we had planned a canyon-run rafting trip through Denali Raft Adventures. The trip promised two hours and eleven miles of scenic adventure through class III and IV rapids in thirty-three-degree glacial waters. We would hit famous runs like "Cable Car," "Coffee Grinder," and "Ice

Worm." We donned drysuits, neoprene boots, life jackets, and helmets over insulated layers. Expectations were running high. Maybe a little too high. While the scenery was stunning and our guide, Jamie, was knowledgeable and a lot of fun, the rapids (given the current flow levels) were a little tamer than what my wife and I, and certainly our two testosterone-laced teenaged sons, had anticipated. It was enjoyable nonetheless and set the table nicely for our first course of Denali.

When we finished rafting, we piled back into the SUV and headed into Denali National Park proper. There is only one road in to, and out of, the park, and, despite that fact, it felt relatively uncrowded compared to places like Smokey Mountain National Park, Yellowstone, or Yosemite.

Denali Park Road parallels the Alaska Range and spans ninety-two rambling miles, snaking through low valleys and high mountain passes. Along its route, beautiful landscapes reveal themselves at every turn, with many opportunities to view Denali — if the normally cloudy skies permit. Wildlife can be prolific, though sightings are not guaranteed — they are, after all, wild animals roaming an unfenced, six-million-acre chunk of public land.

From late May through early September, private vehicles may drive the first fifteen miles of this road to a place called Savage River. Anything beyond that requires a bus. The road to Savage River is paved and features numerous pull-outs to stop and snap pictures. "The Mountain" can be seen as early as mile nine, if the day isn't too overcast — which it is roughly seventy percent of the time. So, that was our plan: drive into Savage River, do some hiking, hopefully see some wildlife, and maybe get lucky enough to be part of that rare thirty percent club.

Our afternoon adventure checked all the boxes. On the drive, we caught quick glimpses of something tall and white peaking above the clouds. Could this be Denali? Arriving at the parking area, we found a trail ascending out of the river valley up to higher elevations and, of course, we took it. Winding higher and higher, the views kept getting better and better. Soon, we spotted a slow-moving bus coming down the road out of the park and, upon further inspection, realized that the bus was following, at a careful distance, a large caribou that had apparently decided the road looked like an easier route than anything else. Eventually, he dropped down into the riverbed and was joined by others. As we kept working our way up, we saw it: Denali, the *Great One*. Completely open and utterly breathtaking. We had officially joined the club.

The next day, on a tip from a seasonal railroad hand, we made plans to take an early morning departure on the Green Bus into the Denali Eielson Visitor Center (mile 66) and back. This was an eight-hour commitment but the only way to truly access the wilder areas of the park, have a shot at seeing more wildlife, and even better views of Denali, weather permitting.

On the short drive from our cabin to the park, a moose

and her two calves lazily fed in a roadside pond just yards from our car. In any other place this would likely cause a pile up of roadside gawkers, but this was Alaska and just another Saturday morning. It's amazing how quickly you assimilate to seeing wildlife in a place like this. Nevertheless, a good omen for what lay ahead.

The Green Bus is very much like a school bus — if the school bus was traveling a gritty single-lane dirt road along steep mountain cliffs into a six-million-acre wilderness and surrounded by things that could eat you. It has seats for two and those sliding windows that go up and down. No food is provided on the trip, so we packed lunches just like those elementary school days. The protocol on the bus is simple. The driver drives, watching for buses coming the other way on the single-lane mountain road, working out, by some mysterious visual cue or secret system, which will slide as far over as possible and which will squeeze past. The passengers alertly watch out the window for wildlife or anything else that might be exciting. Spotting something worthy, you simply yell, "STOP!" The driver will throw it in park, and you can get out (if the situation allows) or slide down the window to take pictures. We were warned ahead of time that there would be abundant wildlife (i.e. don't yell for every caribou or eight hours would easily turn into twelve). At any point during the journey, you could also give a shout and simply get off the bus, wander into the bush, and, hopefully, make your way back to the road later to catch a ride out. For the most part, we opted to stay on the bus and out of the bush until we got to Eielson.

Despite the school bus feeling, the drive is truly staggering as you climb and descend along the dusty road. Through ever-changing landscapes, around blind corners, and over braided rivers. And yes, there was plenty of wildlife. We witnessed numerous caribou and Dall sheep along the first part of the journey, and had our first sighting of a grizzly sow and her cubs a little farther on. Though they were a fair distance away, it was easy to distinguish the size and power of these magnificent creatures from our green roadside perch. Along the way, Denali appeared in several places — larger, whiter, and closer than ever. I fought my urge to yell, "STOP!" at every sighting but had a hard time believing we were going to simply pass by these once-in-a-lifetime views. Nobody else seemed overly concerned, including our driver, so I anxiously bit my tongue, assuming it would somehow get even better.

It did.

As we rounded the last corner to the Eielson Visitors Center, Denali was laid bare before us — no clouds to offer even a scant shred of modesty. I literally lost my breath. I have been all over the country and have seen and hiked in numerous remarkable mountain ranges. I had seen pictures of Denali, read books, and watched documentaries. Nothing prepared me for this. The mountain, all white, appeared like a powerful, resting giant — alive, naked, and breathing, daring any to awaken it.

We left our green school bus and reveled in the magnificence of the vista. Eielson offered the opportunity for hiking both on and off trail. We opted for the Alpine Hike, which travels up Thorofare Ridge some 1,000 feet in two miles. The hike was strenuous on this warm and sunny summer day but delivered breathtaking views of Denali.

When we reached the plateau of the ridge, I stopped to take it all in (and catch my breath) while the boys wandered on a little farther over the green slopes. That moment, that image — my nearly grown sons heading up the viridian hillside, silhouetted, with Denali powerful, majestic, unmovable in stark white contrast behind them — will forever be burned into my memory.

We eventually made our way back down the ridge and wandered a few more trails at lower elevation as small clouds began to clothe the mountain. We ate our lunch in the shadow of the mighty peak, overheard other guests talking about the bears they had run across on their hike, and then boarded a green bus for our ride back. We saw many grizzlies as the afternoon drew on, some as close as fifteen yards. Occasionally, we caught fleeting glimpses of The Great One when we rounded bends. This would be our last night in Alaska, and I could already feel a tinge of sadness, despite such a memorable day.

We slept in a little the next morning, packed up, and prepared to make our way back to Anchorage for the flight home. We made one last drive out to Savage River and were rewarded once again with stunning views and up-close wildlife. Snapshots of Denali faded in the rearview as our time together ended. Overwhelmed by the grandness, wildness, and power of this place and this special time with my family, I grew reflective on how truly diminutive man is and, how, if we choose, blessed we are to have this brief communal with the raw natural world, building memories with those we love.

BONDS OF THE WILD

You hear it all the time: "It goes fast." But nothing can really prepare you for how fast life actually goes. How you can be in your twenties and blink and you're in your forties, blink again and sixty will be staring you in the face. Or how fast the life of your favorite dog passes by, or how quickly your kids grow up — literally before your eyes. It goes fast. All of it.

When I was younger, my thoughts were always on the future, to what would come next. As I get older, more often than not, my thoughts turn toward the past, to memories of days gone by.

What I've never been great at is being in the moment. Being present in what's in front of me right now. Except those times in the wild, away from distractions. Away from the self-inflicted slavery of technology. Away from the to-do list. Away, for the moment, from the pressing and planning and noise and busyness of life.

I've been fortunate to have shared a few of these quiet moments with my dad, my wife, my dog, my close friends, and my two boys. I've been fortunate to have access to relatively untouched places that make these moments possible.

It's a good reminder to savor every single one. To stop, or at the very least, slow down.

To take in a deep breath of the warm spring air. The fresh, rich fragrance of new leaves. The sweet hint of decay in the mud. The fish-and-seaweed aroma of propitious water. The blossoming wildflowers peeking through the cracks in the rocks. The nostalgic scent that only comes from an old outboard or bacon cooking outdoors.

Look around. The morning mist burning off the placid lake at sunrise. The fireflies dancing in the star-filled sky. Look again. The moose tucked just into the brush, that on busier days you would have missed. That contented smile on your loved one's face.

Run your fingers through the cool water. Feel the warmth of the campfire on your bare skin. The rough bark of the logs and the smooth handle of the axe. Savor that venison cooked just enough over the fire. That quick bite on the tongue of your favorite drink. The rich complexity of the dark chocolate that you finally remembered to pack. The morning coffee that ushers in a new day of adventure.

Listen, really listen, to the sounds. The zing of fishing line through the eyelets of your rod. The pop and crackle of the campfire. The distant call of the loon — and the answer. The crickets outside your tent. Tree frogs. The quiet wind brushing gently through the trees. The words of those you share this time with.

These moments, like all moments, are special and will never come again. They are fleeting. Temporary. Living only in memories shared around a campfire in the wild.

TAKING THE BRONZE

Sweat slowly trickles down my back. The thermometer is already pushing ninety, and the humidity is on the rise. Even the beer is getting warm. It's not technically summer for a few days, but someone clearly forgot to tell the weatherman.

Our morning got a late start because Junior had football practice, and it's eleven a.m. before we finally get on the water. The sun is high and the sky clear, not exactly ideal conditions. But I'm glad for the time as days get busier and schedules quickly fill.

It's still prime dry-fly season for trout in Michigan; in fact, even at midday, the air is alive with caddis, drakes, sulphurs, damsels, and even a few dragonflies. But I've decided to haul out the raft and the streamer sticks and chase spawning bronzebacks

Taking the Bronze

on the Muskegon River with my dad and youngest son. We are looking for action, and a serious barroom brawl with something on the other end of a line wouldn't hurt anyone's feelings much either. This group isn't really renowned for their finesse game. The Muskegon River winds its way over 200 miles through the western half of the state before emptying into Muskegon Lake and eventually Lake Michigan. The "MO" is an expansive tailwater and considered by many to be one of the finest fisheries in the Midwest. Several different species of cold and warmwater fish call it home year-round. The prime seven-mile stretch we are floating flows over gravel bars, fast runs, and deep pools.

I've resigned myself to the middle seat for the day, content to watch the guys get after it while I perfect my trademark farmer's tan and stay hydrated.

The action starts slow, and we move more water than fish and put more empties in the boat than bass. We share a few laughs at each other's expense, grab a couple snacks, and reapply sunscreen. But I secretly worry this is going to be a long, fishless float.

We work each section carefully: riffles, buckets, and cutbanks. Testing various patterns (D&Ds, Deceivers, Clousers) in various colors (white, yellow, olive, brown, and black). But still not much action. Finally, we crack the code.

The second strip on the black Sex Dungeon off the shaded bank and Blake is into a really big male that absolutely smashes his fly. We run straight twelve-pound leaders, so there's little worry of a break-off, but this fish intends to let him know he is in a fight. After they go a couple rounds, I grab the net and scoop the thrashing opponent into the boat. He's a solid nineteen. Game on. The mood instantly assumes a more serious tone.

The marathon endures mile after mile, fish after fish. I stop counting after a dozen.

Finally, with just a short bit of the race left, I reach my breaking point. Sliding to the front and entrusting the rowing to my son who has never been described as judicious, I throw caution to the wind and rig up.

My first cast is sloppy, the line wrapping under my foot, while creative expletives travel farther than my fly. A slow, deep breath, and the next cast finds its mark. A quick strip is instantly rewarded with a pulsing rod and a screaming reel. I bring the fish to the boat with shaky hands. I land one more before we take out, and I can't keep the grin off my face. None of us can. It's been one hell of a day.

Trout will always have my heart, and we have plenty of places to chase gold and silver here in the Mitten State; but today I was more than happy taking the bronze.

Going Native

"A spot opened up for the Bowman Island trip."
It's Thursday, February third around 10:30 a.m. when the text from my buddy, Joe, comes through. I'm in the Dominican with my wife and a couple friends, just returning from chasing mahi-mahi the day before, and already a few generously poured Tequila Sunrises deep. Bob Marley is encouraging me to "feel all right," and I do.

It takes a few seconds and all my concentration. "I'm in," I reply as lucidly as possible, desperate to avoid betraying my current, slightly fuzzed condition.

I don't know much about the outing other than it is slated for six days somewhere in Lake Superior near Nipigon, Ontario, and involves chasing overgrown native brook trout, known as coasters, with a fly rod.

Right or wrong, I tend to judge a fishing destination by the level of effort required to get there. Passports, successively smaller planes, distant drives that involve sleeping in trucks, treacherous boat rides, rutted two-tracks requiring chainsaws and winches, or backbreaking hikes with loaded packs, serious elevation gains, and double-digit miles always seem to portend something special.

By those measures, this trip isn't *wildly* exotic, but it's no slouch either, necessitating a twelve-hour drive, travel across the longest suspension bridge in the Western Hemisphere, and a border crossing, all followed by a thirty-mile, four-hour boat ride into the largest freshwater lake in the world — one that has claimed more than 500 ships, including the Edmund Fitzgerald, of Gordon Lightfoot fame.

The Nipigon area itself is steeped in history, deriving its name from a word heard by European explorers when interacting with the native peoples thought to mean "deep and clear water," which it has in abundance.

The first permanent fur trade post was established near Lake Helen on the left bank of the Nipigon River in 1680 and was the center of fur trade until 1775. During that time, the Nipigon District became one of the greatest sources of revenue for traders and produced some of the finest furs on the continent. The last fur trade post, located at what would soon be the Nipigon waterfront, was Red Rock House. It was built in 1859 by the Hudson's Bay Company and burned down in 1891.

Even more importantly, Nipigon is the site of the world-record brook trout — 14 pounds, 8 ounces — caught in the river below Rabbit Falls in 1915 by a Dr. Cook from Port Arthur.

I pull out at ten p.m. sharp with a couple hours of "slush time" built in. Plenty to make the dock pick-up with the rest of the group by early afternoon the following day. I tune in an audio book, lock on the cruise control, and chase sweet-and-sour gummy bears with a lemon Rock Star. Aside from the occasional wildlife it's a quiet, stress-free drive, and I hit the border crossing in the wee hours of the morning, right on schedule.

And that's where I run into my first snag.

I politely hand over my passport and vaccination card to the border agent. A few clicks on the keyboard.

"What is the purpose of your visit, sir?"

"Fishing off Bowman Island. My boat leaves the dock at one p.m."

"This afternoon? Do you know where Bowman Island is?"

"Yes, ma'am."

"Are you vaccinated?"

"Yes ma'am," I reply, showing the beginning stages of annoyance since she is clearly holding my vax card in her hand.

"You're about twenty-one hours early," comes the terse reply.

"What?"

"Your last shot was May 16, which means you can't enter Canada for another twenty-one hours."

"Ma'am?"

"I'm sorry, but you are going to have to return to the U.S."

"Ma'am, I will miss my boat. Is there someone else I can talk to?"

"I'm sorry, no."

"Ma'am, are you *sure* there isn't someone else I can speak with, or a test I can take?"

The sliding window shuts with a metallic clank, followed by a clipped phone conversation, the contents of which I am not privy to. *Good, maybe I can actually talk to someone in charge and explain my situation.*

The window slides back open. "Sir, please pull ahead and to the left under the canopy and wait."

Progress, I think, pulling ahead and parking with a tinge of smug satisfaction.

Moments later, several well-built and equally well-armed men dressed in dark SWAT gear emerge from a serious-looking, windowless brick building and take up position around the 4-Runner. The tinge of satisfaction fades faster than daylight in December, and I roll down the window as commanded by the apparent leader of the balaclava-and-pants-tucked-into-the-boots welcome committee.

"Sir, you need to return to the U.S. immediately; please make your way around the concrete barriers and then proceed left to the border."

I rush off a deflated text: "Stuck at border. Not going to make the boat. Is there a plan B option?"

It's nearly four a.m. when I pull into the only hotel in Sault Sainte Marie that still has a few lights on. The automatic sliding doors bump roughly open, and I'm assaulted by the stale scent of air-conditioned cigarette smoke. The bored manager looks up with a bored expression as a no-nonsense newscaster drones on from the dingy TV in the dingy lobby.

"I need a room, please"

"$130. Check out is at eleven."

You've got to be fucking kidding me. I swipe my card, mount the stairs, and crash — too exhausted for a fight.

Eight a.m. and I'm awakened by the vibrating of my phone. Turns out there *is* a plan B, but it involves Gary, the owner of the lodge, coming back to the mainland in "the big boat" to get me, and it's going to cost about $400 in additional gas. *Shit.* I make the arrangements, and we agree to meet at the docks the next morning.

Using the "level-of-effort-to-get-there" measure, this trip is growing more exotic, not to mention more expensive, by the minute.

Sixteen hours later, and I'm back at the border.

"What is the purpose of your visit, sir?"

"Vacation," I smile, figuring to keep it simple and friendly.

"Are you vaccinated?"

"Yes, ma'am."

"Enjoy your trip."

I've got another six hours to the docks, passing through Wawa, White River, and Marathon, familiar haunts for me, in the dark, as I make my way up the Trans-Canada Highway to the tippy-top of Lake Superior.

I'm a little early, so I pull off at a local diner in a heavy thunderstorm to grab a bite. The place is empty aside from two older gentlemen. I soggily slide into the red vinyl booth behind them.

"Fishing, eh?" the one facing me asks.

"Yes, sir. Chasing coasters," I reply, not entirely sure what gave me away.

"Oh yeah, dos coasters git real big round here, boy." His buddy nods in agreement. "Real big."

My waitress arrives with thin coffee and a pert smile.

"I'll take the bacon and egg special please."

"Sure. And how would you like da eggs, sweetie?"

"Over hard please."

"Oh, well done, eh? And how about your bread, would you like white or brown?"

"Brown," I reply, assuming that's Canada talk for wheat.

"Anything else, hun?"

"Could I get some strawberry jelly for the toast, please?"

"Oh sure, red jam for da toast, you betcha."

My heaping plate of breakfast arrives. Eggs well done, ham

(which is what Canadians mean when they say bacon, apparently), brown toast with da red jam, fried potatoes, and a side of ketchup that, in these parts, goes on everything. I chuckle at the pure Canadian-ness of it all, slice my "bacon," and add a few dollops of ketchup to the eggs and potatoes. When in Rome....

It's still drizzling when I pull up to the docks where I'm met by an easy-going fellow sporting a worn green flannel, dancing eyes, and a wild shock of grey hair that peeks out here and there from beneath a camo ball cap emblazoned with the name of the local hardware store.

"I'm Gary. Let's getcha loaded up."

We stow the luggage and board the *Annica Lee*, Gary's 45-foot, blue-and-white trawler, to begin the next leg of the journey.

A cheery woodstove is burning as I settle in and shake off the wet chill. "There's hot water for coffee down below," he tells me. I duck, make my way under, and pour some Taster's Choice instant crystals into the Styrofoam cup, add hot water, and give it a quick stir while examining the worn nautical map on the wall.

"The boys had a good day yesterday," Gary tells me. "Some nice coasters and a few lakers, too."

He catches my eye and shows me the route we'll be taking on the wall map. "Might get a little bumpy," he warns. "The wind is up, and we've got some weather pushing in."

With a four-hour boat ride ahead of us, I take the opportunity to glean as much inside intel from Gary as possible, considering "the boys" already have a full-day's jump on me.

It turns out this unassuming, 70-something boat captain could easily give the Dos Equis guy a solid run for the "most interesting man in the world" title. Landing somewhere between MacGyver and Indiana Jones, Gary's business card should simply read "Been there, done that."

Several copies of *Scientific American* laying around the boat give evidence to the mind at work. An engineer by background, Gary was employed for many years at the paper mill in Red Rock. He's also been a wildland firefighter, an airplane pilot (and built his own plane), and ship captain (and built, or at least rebuilt the boat we are currently on). The lodge was constructed from lumber that Gary felled and milled himself from the property on which it stands. He's an avid hunter and angler and still runs a trapline every winter, mostly just to stay busy and out of his wife's hair.

Beyond that, he's a wealth of knowledge about the local area and all matters flora and fauna. Gary shares that in the late 1800s, the Nipigon River and nearshore areas were considered the greatest trout fishery in North America, hosting many Americans, Canadians, and even European royalty who came to chase these famous brook trout. But, due to many factors including overharvesting, impeded stream spawning access due to railroad construction, and water level fluctuations from hydrodams that affected trout redds, the population plummeted to the point that in the late 1980s you would be lucky to catch two to three coasters over the course of an entire weekend, and rarely one over a dozen inches.

But the population is on the rebound, thanks in large part to the efforts of Rob Swainson who became the District Biologist for the area in 1988 and made it his mission to restore this important native fishery. And the fishing has gotten really, really, good, Gary assures me. Just last week, he landed a 26-incher right off the dock, he explains, displaying visual evidence via his phone.

The wipers on the windshield slap back and forth, back and forth in the steady rain as we methodically crest and fall, crest and fall over the growing rollers. "There's a bunk down below if you want to get a little shuteye for the last hour or two," Gary tells me, and I take him up on the offer.

I awake in a tangle sometime later, unsure of exactly how long I have been out. Rubbing my eyes, I clumsily make my way up the stairs. "You missed a good one," Gary says, "that was a heck of a storm." The CB radio squawks and a staticky voice crackles through. Gary picks up and answers: "Ya, that was messy, but we made it through okay." Apparently, a neighbor from a nearby island was concerned about our passage. I'm not sure exactly *what* I slept through, but it must have been a doozy.

We round a bend, emerge from a passing fog bank, and eventually make out the lodge, perched on the northernmost spit of Bowman Island. There's action on the dock, and when we finally tie up, I'm met by rest of the crew, which includes Jerry, the trip's host; his friend Bob; a father-and-son duo who have been coming the last few years; my buddy Joe, who is on his first outing; and Bridgette, Gary's trusty Irish setter.

The entire operation is off-grid, powered by solar panels with propane appliances, a wood stove, and running but not potable cold water. There are three bedrooms, a bathroom, a large common room that is open to the kitchen and dining area, a couple small cabins, and a sauna that doubles as the camp "shower."

I quickly unpack and rig up so we can get to the business of throwing line. The fishing here is unguided, with two guys per 16-foot boat, each outfitted with a 40-horse rear-till outboard and depth finder with temperature gauge. The father-and-son team take one boat, Jerry and Bob are in the other, and I'm paired with Joe in the third. The water temp is about 43 degrees. Just a bit cooler than the magic 45-50-degree money zone Gary says we are looking for.

Joe motors to a nearby cove that produced earlier that morning before the storm rolled through. I take the front, attempting to gain my balance while zipping streamers into the shoreline as Joe runs the outboard, doing his best to keep me in position and out of the rocks while dueling the wind and waves. About ten or fifteen casts in and I have my first follow. A quick pause and twitch. The line goes tight, and then starts peeling.

Whoa! The strike is more violent than anticipated, and the relatively small brookie, at least by coaster standards, is working me over like a tomato can. He circles the boat, dives deep, and makes a run before I manage to get him on the reel and work him back close.

"Holy crap!"

"Agwwessive, eh?" Joe snickers with a mouthful of dry Reese's Peanut Butter Cups before grabbing the net. We finally land the fish, probably in the 15- to 16-inch range, and I briefly admire the coveted silvery torpedo before releasing him into the frigid water and switching spots. I'm still shaky from the excitement and beginning to worry I might be a little undergunned with the seven-weight.

We manage a half dozen more between us, all in the 15- to 20-inch range, before heading in for dinner, a hearty moose-spaghetti, and comparing notes with the rest of the crew. By the sounds of it, we all had similar outings, and there were even a couple takers pushing past the 20-inch mark in the other boats. I wouldn't call the fishing easy, especially managing the motor in the wind and waves and making long casts from constantly shifting platform, but the trout certainly seem willing, when we can find them.

Full, feeling a little grubby from my travels and more than a little wind-burned, I decide to "take a sauna," as they say here. Stripping down in the changing room, I slide open the interior door and struggle to catch my breath in the 160-degree wood-stove-heated blast furnace. The "sauna showering" method is relatively straightforward. A tank attached to the stove heats water, and a spigot on the wall provides the cold version; you mix them in a large bucket to an appropriate temperature, grab a ladle, dump-and-lather, then dump-and-rinse.

The evening air feels even cooler now, and I pause on the deck, listening to the haunting call and reply of nearby loons before heading in, cracking a Labatt Blue, and depositing myself on the couch to watch hockey with Gary. Feeling very Canadian at this point, I cheer for Edmonton despite the fact I can't name a single player on their roster.

Over the next several days, Joe and I explore the areas X'd on various camp maps and eventually take to calling them by the local shorthand — The Falls, River Rock, Shoal Breaks, Canadian Camp, The Narrows.

The juicy spots are slowly becoming more noticeable now — like finding the first morel on a spring hunt — and we learn to pass less productive areas while attempting to dodge the never-ceasing "W word" as we've taken to calling it. We work our way around the thickly timbered islands, coves, and inlets looking for the tell-tale drop-offs and structure of the shoal edges, peninsulas, and boulder fields.

Unlike their cousins, coasters seem to prefer sunny

forecasts paired with bright, flashy flies, and collectively we land them in impressive numbers and impressive sizes — the best taping two feet — as the water hits the 45-degree mark and the clouds push out of the system.

Between fish, we watch moose and bear, eagles and loons, and the days run together with the fluidity of waves rippling over rock, each starting with breakfast together and each ending with wild-game dinners, sauna showers, and hockey on the television. Before I know it, the week has passed — like a good hunting dog, well before its time.

I linger a little longer on the deck the last night, smoke my pipe, and gaze into the Canadian sky at stars that seem immeasurably brighter and more abundant than I remember at home, before wrapping up in my sleeping bag on the small wooden bunk for the final time.

We awake the next morning to gloomy overcast skies, the smell of coffee perking, "bacon" on the griddle, and eggs in the frying pan. A quick breakfast before we pack up and head back.

I pour coffee, load my plate with bacon (ham) and eggs, and grab some of the brown toast from the counter. "Can someone please pass the ketchup?"

"Eh?"

"The ketchup please. For my eggs."

Less than a week in Canada, and I already find myself going native.

River Thoughts

I choose to listen to the river for a while, thinking river thoughts, before joining the night and the stars.

If you've spent any time with me at all, you'll understand exactly why I love both this quote and its author, Ed Abbey. River thoughts. Removed from distractions. Left with only the sounds and smells of the woods and the water. The flora and fauna. A rare place where my tangled-in-a-tag-alder mind untangles itself. A place I can turn off forty-two of the forty-three channels simultaneously playing in my head and focus on only one. Where I can pick out the strings section in the symphony of chaos.

Of course, my excuse is fishing. But secretly, I don't go to the river for the fish, I go to the fish for the river. The river that is indifferent to chaos. The fluid medium that understands constant change. Water that is both beautiful and dangerous. That gives life and takes it. The river that is never stagnant. That is born anew after every storm. The river that takes a longer view — not caught in the human immediacy of minutes and hours and days — but lives in the natural world of decades and centuries and millennia. The river that has endured both the insult and the compliment of time. The river that is connected to all things. The life-giving artery of the forest.

When I need to mend myself, I go to the river, cast my problems into its cool steady current, and slowly retrieve its wise reply.

Sometimes I'll even fish. Watching for the slight sip of a crafty trout. Getting lost in the rhythm of the cast. Focused on one seemingly simple task — connecting with something living and vibrant, then releasing it. Letting it go. Giving it back. River thoughts. When the world is too much with me.

William Wordsworth perhaps said it best:

> *The world is too much with us; late and soon,*
> *Getting and spending, we lay waste our powers; —*
> *Little we see in Nature that is ours;*
> *We have given our hearts away, a sordid boon!*
> *This Sea that bares her bosom to the moon;*
> *The winds that will be howling at all hours,*
> *And are up-gathered now like sleeping flowers;*

For this, for everything, we are out of tune;
It moves us not. Great God! I'd rather be
A Pagan suckled in a creed outworn;
So might I, standing on this pleasant lea,
Have glimpses that would make me less forlorn;
Have sight of Proteus rising from the sea;
Or hear old Triton blow his wreathèd horn.

Sometimes I go the river and think river thoughts.

SAWTOOTH

Trudging over the last little rise, the view opened onto a stunningly clear lake dotted with rising trout. Imposing mountains loomed in every direction. A waterfall flowed over a smooth granite face into a deep emerald pool. At that moment, every one of the eight uphill miles and every ounce in my overloaded pack melted away.

We quickly set up camp and began fishing to eager alpine brookies. After a well-earned dinner, we watched the September sun slowly dip behind the ridge from our waterfall perch, and I was reminded of Abbey: "Wilderness is not a luxury but a necessity of the human spirit, and as vital to our lives as water and good bread."

The trip had started with a question: "How are we going

to top this?" We were coming off a backpacking and fly-fishing adventure in Wyoming's Wind River Range, and Max and I were looking for a destination that could keep pace.

It had to be rugged and authentic; big mountains with rivers and lakes were a must. It couldn't be overly touristy and needed to provide ample fly-fishing opportunities. The checklist led to research — scouring blogs, Instagram, travel sites, maps, and books. Locations were proposed. Options were weighed. Emails were exchanged. Finally, we were left with a clear winner: Idaho's Sawtooth Mountains.

The Sawtooths are some of the most stunning and dramatic in the entire country, covering 678 miles and peppered with alpine lakes tucked deep into the high granite peaks and narrow glacial valleys. Our short exploration would barely skim the surface.

We met in Boise, rented a non-descript Toyota Corolla, and drove to Stanley — a quintessential mountain town with dirt roads, wood buildings, and that perfect mix of ranchers, anglers, hunters, river bums, mountain junkies, and the gateway to the Sawtooths. With six days of wilderness on the horizon, our packs felt light as we hit the trail.

After an energy bar-and-coffee breakfast the first morning, we loaded up day packs and fly rods, left camp, and fished our way around the upper and lower lakes. At the eastern end, we discovered a hidden inlet where two mountain streams deposited cold alpine water, creating a sandy flat leading to a deep drop off. I took off my boots, rolled up my pants, tied on an Adams, and fished until my water-numbed legs couldn't take anymore.

Repacking, we followed the stream toward its source. A faint trail headed farther up. Daylight was fading fast. Near the end of the basin, another aquamarine gem lay hidden, high in a protected upper bowl. The mirrored surface perfectly reflecting the peaks' vivid hues. We briefly soaked in the moment then made a hasty retreat back to camp just as the sun began to drop out of sight.

The next morning, before the sun crested the peaks, we broke camp and began our journey — taking a route that traversed a small river and weaved up a breathtaking series of switchbacks. Occasionally the canopy opened, revealing glimpses of the surrounding rims bathed in the soft morning light. We forded the river with only a few mishaps and made our way to the junction.

Now the real work began: the zigzagged trail leading up the mountainside. Our paths crossed a small group of hikers making their way down. They warned of heavy overnight snow but promised that the divide and lakes that lay just over the other side (planned for the next day) were worth the leg-burning effort. Methodically, we made our way up and out of the valley, stopping to rest and take in the views as we went.

When we finally arrived, we were spent and mindlessly set up our tent to settle in. Max grabbed a nap, and I grabbed my fly rod, hustling down to the lake in search of trout. Tired or not, I wanted to get after more fish. I probed along the shoreline, testing different pools that looked promising. As the afternoon rays moved across the sky, light tiptoed over the surrounding mountain spires and brought new depth to the lake as sun and shadow played musical chairs on the surface. I made it back to camp, fishless but content. A full moon above the distant peaks bid goodnight.

At some point that evening, it began to rain. Hard. I wasn't getting wet, so I rolled over and went back to sleep, relatively unconcerned. The next time I woke up, there was water pooling in some areas and running under our sleeping pads. My bag was still dry, so I listened for the rain to lighten as I drifted in and out of sleep and formulated a plan. Gradually, the pelting rain let up. Unzipping the door and peering out, it was evident that the rain had been replaced by a heavy, wet snow. A quick survey of our site revealed ground we thought was high and dry was actually acting as a basin for the standing water and the tent was an island. A classic rookie mistake.

Visibility was terrible, so we scrapped plans for the divide until clouds lifted and provisions dried out. Hanging the gear, we ate a damp lunch. Discouraged. Not too long after, two travelers appeared out of the cloud cover and wandered over. They had been working through the backcountry in higher elevation. Their report of better weather in the forecast lifted our spirits and made the sogginess slightly more bearable. The gear finally dry, we moved camp to higher ground before turning in for the night.

The day announced itself, clear and bitter cold. We ate quickly, loaded frost-covered daypacks and rods, and started up the divide, covering the two-mile ascent in short order. At the top, the view opened to jagged, snow-covered peaks on one side, and deep, cobalt lakes on the other. The morning painted vibrant colors on the granite canvas as we descended the windy switchback that gradually led to the first lake.

Along the way, we scanned the shoreline for signs of movement. Nothing. A feeling of panic began to creep into the pit of my stomach. I wanted fish. We reached the end of the lake and rounded the corner where the second lake lay, much farther below than anticipated.

Descending more switchbacks, my anxious anticipation sat shotgun, making an awful fuss. Following the shoreline to a small outlet, I finally spotted them: stealthy shadows lazing in the shallows, occasionally breaking the surface in quick-feeding splashes. Bingo!

A divide-and-conquer plan was quickly devised. Max would head clockwise around while I worked in the other direction, eventually meeting somewhere in the middle. The shoreline offered very few openings to fish from, but trout were in the water. My adrenaline-fueled eagerness led to several sloppy casts and tree tangles that sent them cruising for cover. I took a deep breath and moved down to a more open section and lobbed a streamer. I was immediately rewarded with a quick strike and soon landed a small, brightly dotted brookie.

Continuing around the shoreline, rings again began breaking the glassy surface. The fish were just begging for dry flies. I switched reels, tied on a trusty Adams, and made the first cast. With a splash, the fly disappeared, and line danced as I stripped in the feisty taker. Holding it momentarily in my hand, I was reminded of a legend which told that brookies had been solid black until a Native American leader named Manitou caught one in his hands long ago. Looking at it, he was struck by its beauty and agile grace and decided to control his hunger and let it live, so he dropped it back into the deep pool. The trout went its way, but instantly its sides took on a silvery hue where the fingers of the Great Spirit had held it, and all its kind became marked with the same silvery sheen and many-colored spots and haloes, as a token of having been handled by the kindly Manitou. It certainly felt like I was holding something that had been touched by a special kind of magic.

I met up with Max, and we fished a little longer. Then, realizing the afternoon was slipping away, we began our return. The valley took on a completely different look now, fading afternoon light casting new shadows and highlighting previously unnoticed beauty. Up and over the top, racing daylight back to camp, making it just in time to watch the sun slowly fade from sight, sharing its last warm, pink light with the surrounding towers.

    Five a.m., one foot in front of the other, down the narrow black trail. The morning eerily silent other than the steady creak of packs and subtle crunch of boots on gravel. The bobbing beam of a headlamp the only illumination. Then the sky, slowly yawning itself awake, transforming from a faint glow on the eastern horizon to a brilliant misty gold. As the morning fog burned off, we paused, watching the sun set the teeth of the mighty saw aflame one last time.

Parts Unknown

"Oh *shit!*" The words erupt spontaneously after two quick strips and a metallic flash engulfs my streamer. The rod pulses wildly as line burns out from beneath calloused fingers. I'm pretty sure I'm into one of the monster smallies this water is known for, until I get another look and realize I'm attached by nothing more than thin, clear gossamer to a trophy brown.

My heart is instantly in my throat, and I can't breathe. Everything else in the world stops. My mouth is dry. My ears are ringing. I keep tension on the rod as the fish runs, heading for heavy water. Back and forth we go. Gaining and losing. A seesaw dance where I swing from lead to follow at the whim of my partner. I'm finally able to work him toward the boat; but we miss with the net, and he's running hard again for the dark current. I'm shaken.

"You're okay. You're okay," Jon encourages. But I don't feel okay. At all. And I make damn sure everyone in the boat knows it. We tango our way through a couple more numbers, and I manage to work him close again; but, seeing the net, he dives, folding my eight-weight in half like an overcooked spaghetti noodle. I'm seeing little black spots at this point. It's total chaos as the net gets frantically passed around the cluttered skiff like a hot potato. The band begins to slow, and once more I bring him close — the net man earning his keep in a quick heavy scoop. I finally remember to breathe. I need to sit down for a second. Reaching for a cigarette, I realize the pack is empty. Cursing myself, I find the closest flask and take a swig. Then another. And another. I'm still shaking. It's not until after the fish is safely released that I'm able to piece together the last five minutes, which seem to have taken place in the third person while I somehow left and then returned to my body. On wobbly legs, I stand and make my way to the middle seat. I'm shot for any more fishing today.

This moment, this collision of circumstances, began a year and a half before when I met Jon Osborn at the Fly Fishing Film Tour in Grand Rapids while manning the Backcountry Hunters and Anglers' booth. We talked for a while, and I purchased his latest book, *Flyfisher's Guide to Michigan*, in which he inscribed the simple words: "Here's to fishing the PM — and parts unknown. Tight lines." Little did I know.

Since that first meeting, Jon and I have developed a friendship, realizing a common passion not only for fly fishing but for fine words laid down on paper and fine bourbon laid down neat, just to name a few. But we had yet to wet a line together. That changed on a warm, partly clouded June day, and I was finally able to chase *parts unknown*, at least to me, with the guy who literally wrote the book on Michigan's fly water. Better still, we are joined by another mutual friend, Jason Veeneman, who spends his days teaching high school history, his evenings building custom bamboo fly rods, and the time in between with prose in hard cover and spirits in brown form. Even if we never move a fish, the day is destined to be a good one.

At this point, I feel compelled (for sake of context) to confess to being someone who values solitude, and I often fish alone. Since we're confessing, I'll further admit at times to being a Plan-A-Creature-of-Habit. For me, there's always something comforting in fishing proven waters where the river bottom is as familiar as an old flannel and the fish lies are as intimate as a faithful lucky hat. But I'm also a restless soul, constantly pulled by the lure of the undiscovered. And, with some newfound time on my hands this season, I dedicated myself to chasing new water with a smattering of friends who I hadn't, for one excuse or another, spent much time with. It was a season for atonement. To move beyond the comfort of the old flannel. It was time to feel the pull of new water and the draw of conversations with someone other than myself.

Our day begins at six a.m. when Jon picks me up. We'll meet Jason north of town at the takeout, spot the car, and make our way. Today, Jon is leading us on his favorite section of river described in his book as "one of the most scenic stretches... in lower Michigan." This water is known to hold trophy-sized browns, hefty resident rainbows, and plenty of outsized bronzebacks.

The ride goes quickly, the conversation ranging from fishing to family to music to books to politics to bourbon and back to fishing while we sip our coffee and the morning dawns. We roll into the parking lot and find Jason waiting, drop the car, and head to the put-in. Right out of the gate the fishing is good. Jason is on the sticks, and Jon and I are moving eager trout with nearly every cast and making good on some of them. We have the river to ourselves, save for an eagle that we bump from perch to perch as we work down the winding waterway in the quietness of the Michigan morning.

Along the way, we stop to switch spots, or take a break and talk, or grab a bite. Our conversation is as fluid as the river and as rewarding as the fishing. Sometimes like the deep outside bends, other times like shallow riffles running over rock. We lose track of time. Our eight-hour float pushing to twelve. Lost in the wonder of new water and the camaraderie of friends who share a passion for wild places.

Only later do I fully realize that *parts unknown* may not even be a reference to a place, but rather to those hidden pieces of myself discovered on a new ribbon of water with friends. Found in the moments that cause me to see things differently, maybe for the first time, because I am finally paying attention. The moments in which my expectations are altered. My views expanded. My senses awakened.

Once again, I feel connected to all things living. The eagle and the trout. The trees and the grass. I gaze into the mysterious water and see myself reflected back. Differently.

LUCKY HATS

Landing the third cutthroat in as many casts offered hard evidence of the omnipotence of lucky hats. On the late-September fishing trip with my dad and oldest son, the faithful camo Simms hat had done its part, producing fish on every river in which it was baptized: the Gallatin, Madison, Soda Butte, Lamar, Firehole, and Gibbon. Now I know what you are thinking: Even a dummy could catch fish in those rivers. But I can confirm that not every dummy on the trip did, and I am convinced it was the hallowed hat more so than my fishing faculties.

Confession: I have a shit-ton of hats. How many is a shit-ton is exactly? A lot. North of fifty. Okay, a hundred. Seriously. Some (my wife) might say it's a problem. Hats on the coat rack, hats in the closet, hats in the other closet, hats in the garage, hats in the truck, hats at the cabin, hats at the family cottage, hats in the office. I am never out of arm's reach of a good hat or twelve. But not all of them are lucky, which leads to another confession. I *may* be slightly superstitious. If something works for me, every effort is made to repeat it with religious fervor *exactly* the same next time. I once had an epic day of fishing on the Pere Marquette River with my buddy who graciously offered the use of his rod and even some of his streamers. The day was so good I decided it needed to be replicated, *exactly*. Later that week, I went out and purchased the exact same rod, reel, line, and streamers. No joke. Or when I've had success hunting, a vigorous attempt is made to reenact the precise particulars perfectly. Same breakfast, same underwear, same socks, same boots, same rifle, same ammo, same jacket, same hand warmers. Same order. Same rituals. You get the idea. And while this practice has met with some success, it doesn't hold as true as hats.

You're probably thinking, coincidence, right? I certainly was, too. Call me skeptically superstitious. But I have tested numerous superstitions and am quick to debunk those that don't hold water. For example, being from Michigan, I am one of those long-suffering Lions fans. Those damn Lions. Many a solemn Sunday afternoon have been sacrificed to my feline friends finding any and every way imaginable to lose a football game. For a while I thought I had cracked the code. I noticed that when I was watching the Lions they would play poorly,

Lucky Hats

and when I wasn't, they would perform better. On the couch with a beer and the Lions find a way to fumble. Get up for a new beer and some chips, they suddenly score 14 points in 34 seconds. Return to the couch, pick six. Coincidence? No, it was clearly a trend. My superstition took over, and I started intentionally *not* watching the Lions play to test the theory. Turns out that while my blood pressure did improve through the process, the Lions actually sucked whether or not I witnessed it. Debunked.

But the hat thing is real. The hat thing is legit.

The real trouble is in identifying the lucky ones — that ageold nature versus nurture debate. While no one will argue that a lucky hat's power increases with age and that you *never ever* for *any* reason wash a lucky hat, I've often borne witness to the "hat is lucky or unlucky from the start" (nature) or the "luck is activated in a hat over time" (nurture) debate. Likely due to my impatience, I have given up on the building-luck-into-a-hatover-time method and find myself firmly in the it's-lucky-or-it'snot-right-off-the-shelf camp.

I've had a few can't-miss hats over the years and currently have two workhorses, but they are getting pretty weathered (not to mention ripe), and it is time to add a few more newbies into the rotation. Some hats just radiate lucky, and that's a solid first step. Next, they need to *feel* lucky. Obviously, not as lucky as they will over time, but I can put on a hat and know if it feels lucky or not. Then comes the true test in the field. A delicate sacrament to say the least. You can sacrifice several good fishing days trying to add a new hat to the lineup. Trust me. My first three outings of the season were blown on this effort to intentionally bring some new hats into the fold. And while I realize this is a long-term investment (a lucky hat can bring several years of good fishing), my next two outings found me in a desperate state, and I went back to one of the trusted starters. And I caught fish, as one would expect.

These are the predicaments that keep a man awake at night.

Poor performers get relegated to the bench (back closet) quickly. Promising up-and-comers get their shot, maybe two if I really like them, but the leash is short. They might end up being a fine grab-a-drink-with-a-buddy hat but never under any circumstances be allowed on a trip to the river. Only the proven veterans earn that honor.

There are some non-believers out there. Some doubters. But this convert will not be found on the river again without my trusted talisman.

I pulled four more cutties out of that hole in four consecutive casts, then handed the rod to one of the unnamed family members on the trip who proceeded to work the spot for fifteen minutes without even a bump. Maybe the fish shut off? As he walked away, I made one more cast, landed one more fish, smiled to myself, and quietly touched the hat in reverent thanks for its service.

I'm a believer.

Five Loaves and Two Fish

I waded into the murky waters of fly fishing later in life. Sure, I grew up chasing panfish and pike with my dad and grandpa, and my wife, boys, and I would throw rubber crawlers for bass at the cottage; but I never had an inkling about pursuing fish with fur and feathers until my older son, Kyle, decided he wanted to learn and requested a rod for his 12th birthday. We set off to test the Pere Marquette River, not far from our summer place in Michigan, so green we didn't even realize how iconic this winding tributary that we'd traveled over so many weekends actually was. He didn't catch anything during those first few outings, and I was relegated to observing from the bank, shrugging my shoulders — no fatherly wisdom to impart.

And then, by complete happenstance, I met a friend of a

friend at a trade show in Chicago. We got talking about kids and hobbies and one thing led to the next. It turned out that her boyfriend was a high-school football coach and avid angler — calling the Pere Marquette his home water. One of his life passions was teaching kids how to fly fish, and she said he would be glad to meet up with us and show Kyle a thing or two.

Meeting Matt quite literally changed the trajectory of our fishing lives. Guiding us to one of his go-to holes on the PM, he instructed Kyle on the basics: finding the risers, determining the proper flies, tying knots, casting, and presentation. Still unsure, I watched from afar — intrigued but not yet infected. As Matt patiently coached, Kyle played the water and, by the end of the night, managed to trick a few small brown trout. The kid was over the moon, and I will have to admit that even I felt a little shaky from the adrenaline of the moment. It became evident that he was a natural, depositing fish in his net on almost every outing thereafter.

The following spring, I was no longer content to be a mere observer — the off-duty lifeguard. This all looked too damn fun, and the competitive side of me was starting to kick in. Like any parent, I enjoyed watching my son's success, but it troubled my male ego to be outdone by the boy. So I pulled a few bucks together and bought my first fly-rod combo from Baldwin Bait and Tackle and ordered a pair of hundred-dollar waders online.

At that point, I didn't know my ass from my elbow when it came to fly fishing (many of my friends would argue, with justified validity, that I still don't), but Matt invited me to join him and a few buddies on their annual spring trip to the Holy Waters of the Au Sable River. I rolled in with my combo set and waders still in the box. No leader. No tippet. No flies. No goop. No knowledge. No shame. And while the other guys made their way upstream to throw something called streamers, Matt helped me rig up and we headed down to attempt what he called swinging nymphs. *Sure, I thought, nymphs sound exactly right in this situation, Matt.*

And then, after what must have been a lot of embarrassing flailing (or what, for me, passed as casting), I actually landed a fish. Holy hell, I couldn't believe it! An eight-inch planter that to this day remains my greatest trophy. At that moment, I unwittingly moved into Stage One of what, in angling circles, is known as the "Five Stages of Fly Fishing" — the pernicious path through the sport from the beginning, where the goal is simply to catch a fish, any fish, of any size, to the end, where you are just damn glad to be fishing, period. Zen-like in its simplicity.

But, like anyone who experiences a taste of success, I wanted more and didn't tarry long in this early stage. The situation spiraled downhill rapidly, and Stage Two developed into a full-blown infection before I could even get a proper diagnosis. I exhibited all the classic symptoms of the "numbers stage," wanting to catch *all* the fish *all* the time, and Matt was more than happy to nurse me through it.

I hit the local rivers with a fervor that would've made a televangelist blush. Fishing whenever I could, with anyone who was willing, for anything that was biting. From blazing hot summer nights chasing smallies to sub-zero winter mornings searching for chrome. As many hours and fish as possible. And you're damn right I was counting; I could tell you precisely how many I had for the evening, for the week, and for the year. My God, I mused, *I am a tremendous fisherman*. Can you believe these numbers? I must be some sort of piscatorial prodigy. Dozens, no, hundreds. Hundreds and hundreds of fish.

Stage Two was spellbinding. But, as man is wont to do, rather than be delighted with some success, I craved more and, almost imperceptibly, slid headlong into Stage Three of the journey.

Stage Three is what I think of as the "Freudian stage," and I suddenly became aware of angler envy. Sure, I was catching a *lot* of fish, but my friends were catching *bigger* fish, and I couldn't help but notice I wasn't measuring up. Regardless of what consoling ex-girlfriends insist, size *does* matter. To believe otherwise would almost be un-American. Super-size it. Hell, colossal size it! Bigger everything. You call that a fish? That, my friend, is bait. All I could contemplate was catching the *biggest* of the big. I'll even admit to becoming annoyed when hooking smaller ones, sometimes secretly resorting to shaking a few off, especially if landing them would mean relinquishing my prized spot in the front of the boat. Awe shoot, I lost him. *Dang.*

Numbers no longer satiated my ravenous appetite. I wanted *monsters*. Trophies worthy of a magazine cover. Trout that broke the 20-inch mark. Soon two feet became the goal, and 30 inches was just around the next bend. And this led to an obsession with streamer fishing, which, to my addled mind, was the *only* proper way to hook the big boys. I quickly outgrew the five-weight, and the six, and, by God, even the seven. *I can't huck meat on anything less than an eight, are you crazy?* I started employing flies whose very names should have been a red flag: Sex Dungeons, Butt Monkeys, and Barely Legals, and never gave it a second thought in the sultry heat of the Freudian stage.

Now, it wasn't *only* about size at this point. For example, plucking a giant out of a stocked pond wouldn't entirely cure what ailed me, but it sure helped stem the bleeding. And catching native fish became more important, not that I could ever get past my obsession with brown trout. And I began to recognize some small satisfaction in pulling off a particularly difficult cast or tricking a more wary fish. I was moving toward Stage Four, but, candidly, it was a case of window shopping more so than full commitment.

Stage Four is best summed up as the "harder is better stage." This sadistic stage forgoes quantity and even size and simply esteems the greatest challenge. Dueling genius-level fish in the *least* ideal conditions. Fun, right?

No. Well, not for me anyway.

I have yet to fully embrace this stage, and I'm quite certain my skill level is a ways off from it even being a consideration. To be honest, I still think of any success in the fly-fishing department as pure dumb luck on my part. Or dumb luck combined with a stubbornness that gets and keeps me on the water as often and as long as possible. Kind of the blind-squirrel-and-the-nut theory. Throw enough bad casts and you're bound to hook into something... eventually. There are always a few gullible fish in most any water.

But I have acquaintances who reside in Stage Four.

Like my buddy Geoff Shirley, who is a dry-fly purist and delights in taking me to some of the most nerve-racking locations possible. Places like Silver Creek, where the fish are so damn smart, the drifts so damn slow, and the microcurrents so damn impossible to read that I didn't dare blink for fear that my presentation would offend these most snooty of trout. He loved it. But it sent me cascading back down the stages like a clown on a unicycle. Big fish? Ha, I could forget about that. Fine, how about lots of fish of any size? Oh, you silly, silly man. Okay, okay, just one fish? Any fish. Please, for the love of God, something! No sir. None for you, you transcendently terrible angler. In fact, it's probably best if you sell all of your gear, torch the waders, and remove any incriminating stickers from your vehicle post-haste; you are an embarrassment to the sport.

Or my friend, Brad Befus, who recently told me, and I quote, that carp are "the best gamefish ever for the long rod." Bold words, Brad. Not muskie or steelhead or tarpon? Do tell. He went on to explain that they are "technical, not forgiving of poor presentation, and just simply hard to pattern." I still didn't see the draw; ugly fish that are really hard to catch... it just didn't have that ring to it. Though I will admit to a passing pang of desire to chase them after this conversation.

Or Landon Mayer. I had the opportunity to spend some time on the water with Landon this past year in Colorado, and let me tell you, this guy *lives* in Stage Four. It was spring and still frosty, with few bugs hatching. The insects that were out were tiny — as in size 24 to 28 tiny. Dust-particle tiny. And the water was low and clear, holding fish sporting IQs in the upper 170s. You could see them, sure, but casting without putting them down was another matter entirely. And this is what he lives for. Tying on microscopic flies with 7X and making perfect drifts to fool spooky fish. I could barely find the fly when I was holding it in my *hand* let alone on the water. And tying on 7X? Forget it. I managed it once, made a few futile drifts with my *Baetis*-shaped dust particle, and gave up. Then proceeded to secure a streamer and flog the water with righteous indignation. But watching Landon do his thing was a work of pure Stage-Four art. I appreciated it but would need many more years before considering taking up residence.

I also had the chance to fish with Jeff Currier last summer. Yeah, *the* Jeff Currier. The one in books and on TV and lecturing around the world. The Catch and Release IGFA World Record holder. The National Fresh Water Fishing Hall of Fame record holder. The one who has well over 400 species of fish on the fly to his name, from parts of the world I can't even pronounce. Exotic fish. Terrifying fish. Gigantic fish. Magazine-cover fish.

But, on a drive out to the Henry's Fork, he shared with me that his greatest catch of all time was an unassuming trout he managed to stalk, pattern, hook, and land while representing the U.S. Fly Fishing Team, leading them to their first ever top-ten finish in the World Fly Fishing Championships in Spain. During the competition, Jeff managed to fool fish on every venue and placed third in the individual standings, becoming the first American ever to take home a medal in the thirty-year history of the Championships. Legitimate Stage Four stuff.

But in Jeff I could also glimpse Stage Five, the stage in which you just want to go fishing. For *all* that it is. The place. The beauty. The quiet. The reflection. Where catching becomes secondary to simply "being."

Now, don't get me wrong, Jeff loves, and I mean *loves*, to land fish. It's heartening to see a guy who has fished for so many years in so many places with so much success still get excited about netting a relatively average cutthroat on his home water. But for Jeff, the joy is in the total experience.

Five Loaves and Two Fish

Stage Five. And I find myself here more often lately. I haven't earned it the way Brad or Landon or Jeff have, and I'll admit to a slight detour around Stage Four, but Stage Five is a fabulous place to spend some time.

There are two key elements to Stage Five — not really their own stages, but additives that make it *even* better.

The first is setting.

I still love chasing big trout and will always prefer lobbing streamers to most any other type of fishing, with terrestrials placing a close second (I'm still not comfortable with subtle presentations and tiny flies — preferring instead something that "plops" when it hits the water). But more and more, I'd take a quiet beautiful place with few other anglers and a couple small fish over a less alluring, and perhaps busier, location that holds bigger ones.

Give me the bucolic beauty of a less popular river in Northern Michigan, or an alpine lake tucked well into the Idaho or Wyoming backcountry, or the small stream in Montana that doesn't get a lot of press but offers stunning vistas, quiet solitude, and every now and then gives up a respectable resident.

Fishing, after all, is a form of escape, and, if that is true, one must rightfully ask, "From what am I escaping?" Noise? Busyness? The modern world? The fast-paced competitive grind of my daily job?

Yes, place *absolutely* matters.

On the opposite side of solitude is the final, and perhaps most important, ingredient, and that is with *whom* I fish. It's like the smoked paprika in a perfect chili. Good without it, but so much better with it.

Like ugly places, I'm just too old to endure ugly personalities and these days prefer the company of those I *truly* enjoy. Unlike in my younger years, the hours and minutes no longer seem limitless. So, the recognition that each one matters — that each grain of sand in the hourglass is precious — makes me carefully consider who I fish with.

I still enjoy chasing blue lines in solitude on occasion, but more often than not, I savor spending these moments in these beautiful places, fish or no fish, with a small circle of close friends and family. Folks who see it the same — maybe not the world, but at least fishing's place in it. And who also understand the delicate balance of solitude and camaraderie. Who no longer feel the need to fill the quiet with empty chatter. Who may, in fact, speak very few words at all. But when we do talk, the conversations are often deep and meaningful or, conversely, light and hilarious — somehow these curated companions intuitively understand what is needed at the moment.

I recently read a Gierach quote: *"I never looked for perfect people to be my friends for fear of going through life friendless. It's just that we get along, see most things the same way, and can disagree peacefully. Some of us can talk politics for hours and get mad as hell,* though not at each other, but with others it's a lot easier to travel and fish together if we don't talk politics, except maybe in the most general terms. I mean the fate of democracy is one thing, but someone you can fish with is another."

And this describes my circle. Not perfect people, *real* people, willing to give some of the sand in their hourglass to another, imperfect person. These friends and family members are multipliers. They capture all that is right about fishing, about being outdoors, and about being alive and then increase it exponentially. Almost Biblical in their ability to take my five meager loaves and two small fish and miraculously materialize a feast fit for 5,000. Or a simple day on the water and compounded it into something even greater than a first fish, a mess of fish, or even a giant. To slow, for a brief time, the sand in the hourglass, and help me see, with a clarity only found on a river together, what really matters.

RETURN TO WIND RIVER

The overloaded pack creaks and groans in rhythm with my labored footsteps. Twelve miles behind and just under two to go. Despite the training, I'm spent. Sitting for a minute, we remove our packs, catch our breath, and rehydrate before pushing on. Making the final ascent, the lake finally comes into view. It's as beautiful as I remember, and the look on my son's face says it all. He gets it. Every mile was worth the effort.

Blake had been asking to go on a backpacking trip for years, and this adventure was months in the planning, retracing a route I'd traveled five seasons before with a buddy. This was an overdue father-and-son outing before my youngest embarked on his final year of high school. By trip's end, we would cover forty-five up-and-down miles in four days, exploring Wyoming's rugged backcountry. Beyond the epic scenery and the fishing, this experience brings a brief respite. An opportunity to escape life's distractions and reconnect with the natural world, building memories and sharing a mutual accomplishment.

I'm eager to drop the pack and ditch the boots, unbuckling and unlacing before we even come to a stop. A flat area with panoramic views provides the perfect place to pitch the tent, unload gear, and grab the fly rods. There's just enough daylight left to get some fishing in, and we intend to make the most of it. There's a spot a mile or so from camp, and I'm anxious to see if it still produces. We land a couple.

I take a pull and pass the flask. Neither being much for words, the satisfaction of the moment remains unspoken but silently understood. Thoroughly exhausted, we head back for a quick dinner before bidding goodnight to our first day.

Sore bodies make for restless sleep, and we're up with the warming sun. Finishing a hasty breakfast, the fishing gear is gathered for the day's outing. Today we're exploring four miles of new contours and blue lines on the topo, and expectations run high.

According to the map, the lake drains into a river system, feeding another smaller lake and another and another. We head out, finding runs brimming with small waterfalls, bubbling riffles, and deep pockets. It all looks fishy, and it is.

We spread out, working various lies and holes with dry

flies and small streamers, catching our fill of bright, hard-fighting cutties and bows. Each returned with a splashy farewell. After working down about four miles, we turn and fish back up. Despite the bright day and clear water, we manage to land a few dozen fish.

Nearing the top of the outlet, the weather takes a mountain turn, and, for a short window, heavy drops of sleety rain pelt down relentlessly. Junior lets out a sharp holler, suggesting he's into something a little more serious. Rushing over, I quickly dip the net and pull up one of the most beautiful trout I have ever laid eyes on. Wearing the telltale bright spots and vibrant halos, I'm reminded of a quote from Cormac McCarthy's *The Road*: "*Once there were brook trout in the streams in the mountains. You could see them standing in the amber current where the white edges of their fins wimpled softly in the flow. They smelled of moss in your hand. Polished and muscular and torsional. On their backs were vermiculate patterns that were maps of the world in its becoming. Maps and mazes. Of a thing which could not be put back. Not be made right again. In the deep glens where they lived all things were older than man and they hummed of mystery.*"

Released back to his watery abode, I'm grateful for a life that still affords such mysteries.

Sunburned and satisfied, we head back to camp to discuss plans for tomorrow over a simple meal and a few games of cards. But sleep overtakes us, so we call it a draw and switch off the lantern.

Sipping fresh morning coffee under a cloudless sky, we fuel up for the day's eight-mile roundtrip. The trek promises some of the most spectacular scenery so far and, if luck holds, a repeat of yesterday's fishing. The morning hike starts cool and comfortable, and we make good time. Wildflowers line the path, painting the harsh landscape with cheerful yellows, reds, and purples. A juxtaposition only nature could write with a straight face.

A deep, blue pool below a fractured waterfall offers our first glimpse at fish, large and actively feeding but very spooky. We cast over them for a long time, offering everything in the fly box, but never close the deal. It foreshadows the rest of the day.

Soaking in the breathtaking scenery under a warm blank sky, we lick our wounds from being bested before turning back to retrace the route. Unwilling to admit defeat, I suggest a slight detour on the return, opting to fish the base of a giant waterfall across the lake from our campsite. We deliver a grand effort, but our fate has clearly been sealed; we head back to camp humbled and utterly fishless.

We take our time the next morning preparing to hike out, budgeting two days for the journey if needed. After breakfast, we slowly pack up and get on the trail, retracing day one in reverse order. With miles ahead, we're stalling, delaying the inevitable.

But we make good time and decide to push all the way, covering the thirteen-mile trek in just under six hours. At the trailhead, sweaty packs are triumphantly offloaded on the tailgate, and the accomplishment is celebrated with another pull from the flask, reminiscing on the last four days of adventure.

A cheap hotel, warm showers, and fresh clothes are all welcome luxuries. Splitting a pizza in town, Blake talks about plans to return with his buddies to hit a few unexplored lakes. I'm thankful for this time together — and that Blake's thirst for adventure has been properly primed.

Because of the early push out, we have the entire day to fish and explore back to Jackson. After a questionable hotel breakfast, we swing by the local fly shop to verify plans and dig up any intel they are willing to offer.

With a little coaxing, the kid behind the desk quietly surrenders inside information on some small water way up in the national forest. We hit the road armed with small streamers, Yellow Sallies, and grasshoppers, and find eager native cutthroat in every run. After catching our fill, we're back on the road and wader-up for some bigger water and more cooperative fish. It seems the curse has been broken.

Nearing the city, it becomes busy, and the adjustment is jarring. After short showers at the hotel, we head downtown for burgers. The sun is starting to set, so we finish up quickly before driving out to a roadside pull-off to watch the day come to a close over the towering Tetons.

Boarding the plane the next morning, our trip ending before it even seemed to begin, I'm reminded how quickly eighteen years can go. I stop, take one last picture, and relish the view. Looking over at Blake, I catch a rare smile. And then I know, at that very moment, we are both planning our return to Wind River.

Fall

A lone leaf spirals
To the ground in one last colorful dance.
Far off, the pulsing drum of a partridge cuts crisp air.
Filled with the scent of mossy decay and damp wood smoke,
The forest comes alive as morning shadows give way.
I grab my bow and follow the oak ridge.
It's fall…

AN ODE TO SHASTALAND

Michigan offers an embarrassing bounty of public wilderness to hunt, fish, and otherwise recreate on, but since a young age, I had always longed for a small piece of land we could call our own.

Together, my dad and I made hunting day trips, sometimes stayed in campers and tents, joined friends and family when the invites came, and eventually took to renting a cabin each October, but I was always looking. Dragging him to various pieces of property, we would dream about how we would hunt it, where a cabin might go, and the perfect place for a fire pit. But it was never really in the cards.

As the years went by, the dream seemed less likely as I became busy with work and starting a family, and dad worked his way toward retirement. My two boys became part of the equation, and as soon as they were old enough, they joined us on our hunting and fishing adventures, staying in the rented cabin, exploring the woods, throwing lures to fish, sharing stories around the campfires, playing card games by lantern light, and practicing with toy bows. They grew to love the outdoors and this special place we returned to every year as the leaves began to turn. But the dream of our own little piece of land never left. In fact, it grew stronger.

When the boys were old enough to actually start hunting with us, we would take turns with them in homemade ground blinds, building up the patience required to gain success. Eventually they joined us in the trees, and we would set up stands in nearby hardwoods to supervise and make sure they stayed safe. It was rewarding to see them grow and develop as hunters. We built memories, to be sure, but day trips became difficult and we could only rent the nearby rustic cabin one weekend per season. I wanted more. More time together. More space to spread out. More opportunities for the boys. I quietly continued the search for a place of our own.

By 2012, my longing had reached a fever pitch as I realized how quickly the boys were growing up. They would turn 10 and 12 that year, and I could feel the moments accelerating by. With the added constraints of sports schedules, we were losing time. I began my search in earnest and persuaded my wife to buy-in to the idea, at least in theory. Which was close enough

An Ode to Shastaland

for me. I scoured property listings, picked up local real-estate magazines, and visited websites. I knew that I would want at least enough acreage to hunt, but it needed to be in close proximity to public land as well. If it offered nearby fishing opportunities, that would be an added bonus. I dragged my dad to various properties — looking at small parcels with old cabins and remote chunks with more acreage. The boys tagged along to look at other pieces and plots when dad wasn't available. I was on a mission. We walked a lot of land. But none of these places felt right.

Then I saw an ad for three twenty-acre parcels in Cadillac, only about six miles from my buddy's hunting camp and the public-land hills I had been successfully gun-hunting for the last several years. The parcels fronted a paved road and backed up to thousands of acres of federal property near some great fishing lakes and rivers. They offered an intriguing mix of young pines, berry bushes, hardwoods, open areas thick with ferns, and cedar swamps. So I ditched work, hopped in the truck, and made the drive. I had an old pair of shorts in the backseat (in case of emergency) and a pair of sandals. I quickly changed out of my work clothes and started to walk the property. It felt right. An older tree stand in the hardwoods confirmed that someone had, at some point, deemed this area worth hunting. Deer and bear tracks pockmarked the softer ground, and I jumped a doe and her fawn in the ferns. I knew this was it. I got home that night, my legs covered in scratches from my shorts-and-sandal adventure, and had a little explaining to do with my wife.

In the end, Joy gave me the green light to continue the process, so I called the realtor for more details. And then I called my dad. I wanted him to walk this property with me to see if it felt right to him, too. We drove up together and walked the land. He felt it. All sixty acres would have been nice, but the wife-approved budget only allowed for twenty, and we knew which parcel we wanted.

We were set to close in early September, and I wanted to get the property ready for the youth hunt a few short weeks later. We placed a handful of stands carefully around promising areas of our new property. In the meantime, I worked feverishly to acquire more gear. I bartered, bought, and traded for trail cameras, additional stands, ladder sticks, picnic tables, and even a beat-up old Yamaha Blaster that we could bang around on. But my biggest obsession was finding a place to stay on the property. The area offered cabins for rent nearby — but that just wouldn't do. I wanted something of our own. I obsessed over it, sending my dad links to various "deer-camp-special" campers that I wanted him to buy (I was out of cash at this point). I was finally able to convince him with a 1973, 28-foot Shasta camper that didn't look too horrible. Some minor damage, a leak here and there, a flat tire, a broken taillight — no worries. Dad floated the cash, and my buddy Jeff and I went to pick up the new cabin on wheels. We had to pump the weather-checked tires up to make the trip — three of them mostly held air. We drove it back to the house to clean it up some, the awning falling off on the way. A few zip ties and bungies and we were back on the road — again, no worries.

I convinced Jeff and another buddy to help me tow the mostly road-worthy camper up to the property. Somehow it made it, and we celebrated the new lodging with a few beers while I surveyed the kingdom. We had our basecamp.

The Shasta could sleep my dad and I and the two boys — kind of. Dad commandeered the table-turned-bed near the "kitchen" while Kyle and I claimed the two benches around the front table and Blake took the fold-down bunk above the table. Since we didn't have running water, the back of the camper (previously the bathroom) became our storage area. We'd eat outside on a $25 picnic table or, in bad weather, the front table while sitting on the "beds." It was a little tight, leaked some, and didn't really hold any heat (something discovered later in the season). We would use lanterns for light and did our best to keep the brown shag carpet clean-ish. We didn't care. The Shasta was our weekend home, and we felt like kings.

We worked that twenty-acres, developing food plots (still a learning process); the boys (yes, all of us) blazed trails, cut firewood, ate horrible food, practiced with bows and guns, rode quads, sat around campfires with friends, harvested morels, played games, built forts, fished nearby lakes and rivers, occasionally hunted, and mostly just enjoyed having our own place together. Laughter was our currency. My friends and family took to calling the place Shastaland after that old camper, and the name stuck.

The fifth season on the property, we finally harvested our first deer — a small buck that my younger son took during the youth hunt. Sure, we'd seen a bunch of others and passed on a few, but Shastaland had never been about deer in the freezer.

While my kids' earliest hunting memories will always be attached to the public land we first explored together and the rustic cabin where we gathered once a year, Shastaland became our own little sanctuary — a place much longed for. A place we could call our own and where we could all be kids again.

THE LESSONS OF SILVER CREEK

I wasn't ready for it. I can see that now. Not just the beauty of the place, but the place itself.

In fly fishing, some waters are legendary. The Henry's Fork, the Yellowstone, the Colorado, the Platte, the Madison, the Beaverkill, the Deschutes, the Kenai, the Holy Waters of the Au Sable. Silver Creek certainly has a place on that list — probably pretty close to the top. This is hallowed ground where Ernest Hemingway, Bud and Nick Purdy, and countless other famous fly anglers cut their teeth.

While I became a disciple of fly fishing later in life, I've had the opportunity to fish several of these sacred places. Others remained on the bucket list. Silver Creek was on that list until a few Septembers back, when I got my opportunity.

Flowing at the base of the Picabo Hills, this high-desert spring creek attracts an abundance of wildlife including eagles, waterfowl, coyotes, bobcats, mountain lions, deer, and elk. Silver Creek's unique aquatic ecosystem features one of the highest densities of stream insects in North America, which support a world-class fishery. It's a place where you can immediately feel the presence of your predecessors.

It was evident the moment I took my first tenuous steps into the clear, slow water, like one of the uninitiated stepping into a holy temple. It was evident as the sun slowly dipped and painted the mountains a vibrant pink, filling the valley with an impossible light. It was evident as dainty mayflies darkened the sky and noses began to quietly break the surface without as much as a ripple. As I slowly unfurled my line and cautiously made my first cast, hitting my mark, only to be less-than-politely refused. This intimate river was not a place for those without battle scars, unending patience, and a little grey hair. I had been warned.

In hindsight, the silver around my temples and the success I've enjoyed in other water perhaps made me a little too confident. Despite my age, I still fly fish like a young dog hunts. I can't help it. The adrenaline gets the best of me. I'm too eager, too aggressive. I favor streamers, large terrestrials, and mice. I don't think the 6X tippet has ever left the spool. Like a teenage boy on a first date, I had come to Silver Creek clumsy, unsure, and filled with desire. I learned the hard way.

But like special people and special places, certain rivers change you. Silver Creek wasn't a cheap beer to chug; it was a complex Bordeaux meant to be savored, appreciated, sipped slowly. It was a good lesson for fishing and an even greater lesson for life.

I'll be back to Silver to be sure, when I have a few more gray hairs and battle scars. When I'm able to hunt like a more-seasoned dog. When I've learned to better manage my fish lust. At my age, it's important to have ideals that are still unattainable. That challenge you. That give you something to look forward to. Something still unspoiled and left to the imagination.

Yellowstone

It was supposed to be a hunting trip.

My oldest son, Kyle, had moved to Bozeman in 2018 to attend college, and since then, my dad and I had been planning a backcountry Montana muley hunt for the three of us. While I had already found reasons to visit, this was going to be Dad's first time. We'd drive to Bozeman, grab the boy, and hit the boundless backcountry — hunting, camping under the stars, telling stories around a campfire, struggling under heavy packs coming out. Glorious.

And then around mid-summer, I received a letter in the mail from Montana Fish and Wildlife — a check actually. A refund for my permit and an explanation that I had not been drawn for a hunt. Better luck next time. That added a small

Yellowstone

wrinkle into things. Time to develop Plan B.

In truth, Plan B was pretty easy. I had been able to fish Montana several times but had never fished in Yellowstone. It was a bucket-list trip, and this was the perfect opportunity. The stinging disappointment of a missed hunt was quickly replaced with the gratifying anticipation of a fly-fishing adventure in America's oldest national park. We would target the end of September, hoping to cash in on terrestrial season and possibly intercept a few large pre-spawn browns and native cutthroat.

The research phase began in earnest. We contacted friends, read books, consulted maps, purchased plane tickets, and booked cabins. The itinerary emerged pretty straightforward. We'd fly into Bozeman, hit the Gallatin that afternoon, bunk at my son's house, and get up early the next morning to make our way to Cooke City-Silver Gate, just outside the Northeast entrance. Then we'd fish the park for three solid days and part of a fourth as we worked our way back. Simple.

The first part of the trip went exactly as planned. We met Kyle at the airport, loaded gear, purchased licenses, and made straight for the river. The weather was perfect, and the Gallatin was feeling generous that afternoon. We landed a number of chunky browns and topped the night off with pizza downtown. Everything was off to a perfect start. But as often happens with these types of trips, things changed.

Kyle ended up having a test he couldn't miss the next

afternoon, which left an entire day open. Beyond that, the news reported weather rolling in that threatened to shut down the terrestrial fishing and, even worse, the roads into and out of the park.

Dad and I decided to try our hand at the Madison near West Yellowstone while Kyle finished class, and then grab him and make our way to our remote cabin for the night — weather permitting. With the dire forecast, we weren't sure what to expect, but the weather gods smiled on us, even if the fishing deities didn't. We caught a few mid-sized browns but mostly just enjoyed a beautiful day in beautiful country.

Heading back to Bozeman, the weather started taking a turn. We picked up Kyle and began the journey to Silver Gate. I'll admit now that I *seriously* underestimated this drive. Paradise Valley was socked in, and we slowed to a safe crawl. Entering Yellowstone through the north entrance, we white-knuckled it through the park, navigating slippery roads and dodging wildlife in the dark. We finally made it to the cabin well after midnight and fell asleep immediately upon hitting the beds.

A light dusting of snow and breaking cloud cover greeted us the next morning. After grabbing a quick breakfast, we were off for a day of fishing the Soda Butte and the Lamar. Kyle had a spot he wanted to hit first — a productive pool he had found earlier in the season that required a short hike in.

We scouted the location. The river was up a little and

slightly stained, but the pool looked fishy as hell. The best way to approach it, he instructed, was from a large boulder just upstream. I must have looked anxious (or maybe stupid) because I was given first pass. I gingerly navigated the slippery rocks up onto the boulder perch to study the current, visualizing exactly how to play my streamer through the run. With great anticipation, I stripped out line and fired a cast, realized some of the line was underfoot, tried to readjust, and quickly found myself ass over applecart off the back of the boulder. And, just as quickly, straddling another large rock, neither foot touching bottom, sunglasses gone, and line tangled in a giant bird's nest.

Laughter and taunting quickly ensued. While I untangled my mess and my pride, Kyle added insult to injury by executing a single surgical cast into the pool and hooking a nice fish within seconds of his streamer hitting the water. At that point, it is possible that I blacked out from rage because the rest is a little blurry.

Somehow, I got a second chance. Perhaps it was fear-induced but more likely a gesture of simple pity. Or, perhaps Kyle and Dad just wanted to see more river acrobatics. Either way, I was glad for the opportunity and elected to use the "shore method" this go-round. On the third cast, my streamer disappeared in a violent slash, and I redeemed myself — at least for the moment.

After a few incredible hours on the Soda Butte, we decided

to try our luck on the Lamar. Loading back into the truck and through the Lamar Valley, dodging bison along the way as the weather cycled from rain to sun to hail and back to rain. The Lamar is a beautiful river that looks and fishes differently than the Soda Butte. It took a while, but once we figured it out, a number of respectable cutthroat found the net.

The next day presented a bit of a navigational challenge. The plan was to hit the famed Firehole and the Gibbon, but that meant traveling from the far northeast corner of the park to the deep southwest corner. In normal conditions, this would be a relatively easy, albeit somewhat slow, drive. But we had to wind up and over Dunraven Pass. So far, we had gotten pretty lucky with the weather, but this would be the real test.

We eventually made it over the pass, finding Mother Nature's mood on the other side a little more forgiving. Now for the Firehole, a river that one friend described as an almost religious experience. He wasn't wrong. Imagine fishing a pristine, gin-clear river on a strange and somewhat barren landscape while steam rises all around and buffalo graze alongside. It's truly impossible to properly describe in words or in pictures – the closest I can come is otherworldly.

The bed of the Firehole is very different than other Western rivers. Instead of sand, gravel, or slippery boulders, the bottom is mostly volcanic rock. And, because the river flows through several significant geyser basins and is surrounded by geothermal features, the temperature runs significantly warmer than some of its sisters. It all combines to create an extremely unique fishery.

We started throwing streamers with marginal success, but soon saw the water dimpled with rising trout and the air dotted with small bugs. Time to switch to dry flies. Kyle, who by my own admission has a much better dry fly presentation than me, was landing fish after fish. Meanwhile, Dad and I got blanked despite offering up the same menu items. I was not impressed.

The weather was getting pretty ugly. A stiff wind was hurling a cold rain, but we still wanted to fish the Gibbon. So, we found a pull-off, hiked in, and made a half-hearted attempt. Hands numb from the cold, we landed a couple small cutties and cutbows and crossed it off the list.

The weather grew worse the next morning. A heavy wet snow was falling, and Bozeman was still a long drive away. The original plan was to fish through the park on the way back, but given the weather conditions, we decided to stop in town for a quick breakfast and then get on the road home as early as possible.

The route through the park was slow and more than a little sketchy. Narrow, snow-covered roads mixed with poor visibility, wandering wildlife, and steep grades made for adventurous travel even with four-wheel drive. After seeing a few cars ditched off the side, we elected to skip fishing on the way back and take our time getting through the weather, occasionally stopping to photograph bison cloaked in white blankets.

We made it back to Bozeman by early afternoon, the weather gradually improving along the way, and decided to hit the Gallatin one last time before calling it a trip. Kyle mentioned a sneaky spot that typically held good fish, and, despite the cold, a few were willing to play. We ended the evening back at his house dealing cards and sharing stories around the table, sad that our time together was coming to an end but grateful for every moment.

On the plane ride home, it struck me that a lot of things on this trip didn't go exactly as planned. Then again, chasing new wilderness and new water, encounters with incredible wildlife and fickle mountain weather, stories of lost fish, lost sunglasses, and lost rods, and bruises in a few tender spots, left us feeling connected and alive. And that is all anyone could ever ask.

Michigan Escape

Swollen raindrops ping on the metal roof of the cabin, like dimes being dropped on the wood floor, and the old gas lantern, with its steady hiss, envelopes the small space in warm light. Soothing. Peaceful. A cool October evening in northern Michigan. My only company is Harrison in hard cover, Jameson in a tin cup, and thoughts of tomorrow's float down one of my favorite rivers with a friend. I finish my drink and my chapter, extinguish the lantern, and turn in for the evening. The rain's staccato storytelling and the tangy smell of cut pine boards on the walls my last cogent memories.

As the morning yawns itself awake, I can hear that the rain has let up. Shaking loose from the sleeping bag, I get some coffee started in the camp percolator — the one that always reminds me of my grandparents' house during the holidays. I fill the trusty red thermos, throw on an old flannel, and hit the road. The damp holds promise. The promise of escape. The promise of the river. And perhaps, if luck holds, the promise of a fall brown trout on the fly.

A Dierks Bentley song playing on a local country station feels especially poignant in the moment — like a short sermon delivered to a delinquent parishioner: *"This morning I got up at 6:01. I walked out and saw the rising sun. And drank it in like whiskey. I saw a tree I've seen a thousand times. A bird on a branch and I watched it fly away in the wind. And it hit me. It's a beautiful world sometimes I don't see so clear."* The tires hum along the worn blacktop. I sip my coffee and observe the passing landscape with newfound appreciation, the message having found its mark.

Pulling into the vacant boat launch, cold gravel crunches under the tires. I see Geoff, already in his waders, looking out over the tannic ribbon of water. Colored leaves rattle quietly in the trees. It's a distinctly Michigan fall scene. The breeze carries a hint of decay as one season transitions to the next — birth to death, death to birth. I walk up beside him and pass the thermos as we watch the river.

Moving now, the oars dip quietly into tea-colored water that pulls ever forward, the calmness of its surface belying the turbulence below. The stillness is so complete that, for a time, we merely glide along, afraid that even the gentle whisper of fly line will offend the moment.

Eventually, we mingle into the rhythm of the stream, and out of habit, I adjust the weathered camo hat on my head hoping to coax a small measure of the luck it holds. Pulling back gently on the oars — already fighting the inevitable end — I move the boat into position. Geoff's cast finds a promising undercut bank on the left, seasons of practice displayed in a tight loop. A slow twitch followed by a watery explosion and the hat has done its job. I smile knowingly to myself and grab the net.

Another sip from the thermos, and we continue down the winding waterway like time itself. My tired soul rejuvenated by the incomparable beauty of the feisty spotted fish, the light gurgle and bubble that gently eases us along, and the heavy scent of wet leaves hanging like gaudy ornaments in the trees. I'm buoyed by the friendship, powerful in its quiet way, and the knowledge that escape is only ever as far away as a river with a friend and a thermos of warm coffee.

My Uncle's Farm

Fire and smoke poured out the end of the barrel, and the deer quietly fell as the rest of the group moved quickly on. The smell of spent gunpowder hung heavy in the cold air. Rapid breaths frosting the scope. I began shaking, finally realizing the true cold and the weight of the moment. My first buck.

Dad had been taking me hunting since I was 12. Bow hunting mostly. In the early days, we hunted off the ground on a tract of land owned by Consumer's Power that they made available to the public. Looking for runs and making ground blinds out of fallen branches, sitting as long as a youngster could in the hopes of catching some passing deer. We didn't see a lot in those early days, mostly, I'm sure, due to lack of skill. As the years went on, success gradually followed. We moved off the ground into tree stands. We explored religiously and learned the terrain intimately. Books, articles, and videos were scoured, and young patience lengthened a little each time out. Eventually, venison started filling the freezer. It was good.

Then the opportunity came. The invite to hunt my uncle's new 140-acre farm in the middle of the state on the holiest of hunting days, November 15 — the opening of Michigan's firearm season. The farm was loaded with deer. Big ones. I couldn't sleep for weeks with anticipation.

The loaded truck rolled out after dinner on the 14th, the evening spent on a couple of couches by the woodstove waiting for the approaching morning. Sleep was once again hard to come by. Finally, the hour arrived and my uncle came to wake those of us who actually slept (Dad).

I was young and broke in those days and didn't even own a rifle, so my uncle loaned his Remington Woodmaster to use for the hunt. It was beautiful. Rich wood and a glossy finish with engraving. It looked like the pictures in the catalog. I was familiar with firearms, but he carefully showed me how the magazine worked, assured me that the scope was dead-on, and had me shoulder the unloaded gun to get a feel. It was solid and heavy and serious and smelled of gun oil — a scent that, to this day, brings me back, like coffee brewing by the fireplace at my grandparents' house or a freshly unwrapped pack of baseball cards with the stale pink gum.

We quickly dressed and headed out to our respective spots.

I was awarded the prime location — a small rise on the edge of the bean field. Dad was posted at a cut that ran between two wetland areas, and my uncle would be watching an area of woods that bordered some cornfields. The morning was crisp and very cold — the hard frost crunching under thick boots as I made my way out to the blind. I sat in the dark shivering, partly from the cold but more from the anticipation.

Ever so slowly, at an almost imperceptible pace, the blackness turned to grey and the landscape began to take shape. Deer started moving. Running. It was still too dark to shoot, but two bucks had already passed by at less than forty yards. It all felt like an incredible dream that I didn't want to wake from.

As the morning began to break and the sun began its slow ascent, I sat. Rigidly waiting. Cold. With every nerve tingling and every sense on high alert. And then, there! Out of the corner of my eye far to my left, a group of seven deer were making their way out of the morning fog in my direction. It was clear that three of the seven were bucks, and big ones — especially to a boy who had never wrapped his hands around antlers of his own. I pulled the rifle up and followed the group as they worked into range, trying to slow my racing heart while warm breath frosted the scope lens. They were coming. Moving off the scope to get a better look, I picked out the biggest of the three bucks while letting the frost clear. Moving my cheek back down to the rifle, I found my deer in the glass, settled the crosshairs right behind his shoulder, clicked off the safety, and slowly squeezed the trigger. It happened so quickly and so slowly at the same time.

Heart pounding, ears ringing, and body shaking, all I could do was wait. So, I did. After what seemed like hours, but was likely only ten or fifteen minutes, I gathered myself and walked out. My first buck. A pounding heart and the crunching of boots on the frosty ground was the only interruption to the silence that had once again fallen upon the morning. With some trepidation I approached the animal — experiencing the mixture of raw sadness bordering on guilt and pure jubilation that only a hunter understands. I laid my shaky hands on his still-warm body and silently paid my respects.

The excitement was barely containable, but this was well before cell phones or texting and we didn't even have walkie-talkies. Worse yet, it was still prime hunting time — barely a half hour into shooting light. I didn't want to screw up my dad's hunt, but I really couldn't wait any longer. I slowly made my way over to the cut where he was sitting. He waved and waited with a smile — the excitement on my face clearly evident. He wasn't mad, in fact, he was really excited, a feeling I now understand as a father myself. Together we walked over to my deer — a tall seven with two tines broken off earlier in the season — and he congratulated me with a handshake turned hug. My uncle must have recognized the shot because he soon appeared over the hill and helped finish the field dressing. Beaming with the pride that his land, his gun, and his blind had delivered for his nephew.

Back inside, we celebrated with a hot pancake-and-bacon breakfast, the morning hunting still in its prime but content to enjoy the moment together. Just then, I spied a huge buck making its way up the cut my dad had been sitting in. I pointed excitedly, and my dad just chuckled while my uncle raced for the door, forgetting his boots but grabbing his .270 on his way out. We didn't get that giant, but I will never forget him or that that day: the smell of the gun oil, the crunch of boots on the frozen ground, the deer magically appearing out of the fog, the hot breath frosting my scope, and the time with my dad and uncle in celebration.

My uncle no longer lives on that farm, but that .308, well, I saved up and bought it from him and then passed it on to my oldest son to harvest his first buck. And we still spend hunting seasons together sharing stories around campfires. It all comes around, and moments like these remain dreamlike, even as life hurries by.

ECHOES OF THE FOREST

A light snow begins to fall in the forest. Coming to rest on the boughs and carpeting the now brown pine needles and shriveled ferns. Blanketing the landscape in white silence. In my periphery, I sense movement. Slowly turning to see legs moving surreptitiously between young trees. A few more moments. I watch intently as the buck takes three cautious steps into the small opening. Rifle comes to shoulder, and a single shot breaks the silence, echoing as he falls. By many standards, he isn't huge, but he is a trophy to me, not only for the food he will provide my family for the coming months, but also because he was taken in a place I love. In an annual gathering of people I love equally.

I've always preferred the woods. I love mountains and

oceans. There's something magical about open prairies. I find solace in rivers. But for me, I'm most at home, most alive, in the woods. I long for oak ridges and pine stands. The damp musk of cedar swamps. The brilliance of maples and the smooth strength of beech. The slashings of aspen and poplar and the bleached bark of birch.

I owe these passions to my father. To the seed he planted long ago and then painstakingly watered to fruition. For as far back as I can remember, my extended family camped every summer and fall in the wooded lands of northern Michigan. And I still get nostalgic for the smell of camp in the morning — coffee brewing and bacon cooking with a side of wood smoke. And, because of him, I was introduced to hunting when I was 12. He helped me save my paper route money for my first bow, bought me my first camo from the K-mart "up north," and gave me my first pocketknife. Then spent endless patient hours walking the woods and sitting in blinds with me. I, in turn, have done what I can to pass these passions and traditions on to my two boys. Many of my most-favored moments have come outdoors, in timbered groves, with my father and sons and friends. And maybe that's the reason. The forest holds memories. Holds history and meaning. Just like the stories held in the rings of every tree.

In his memoir, *Off to the Side,* Jim Harrison penned an incredibly powerful chapter entitled "Hunting, Fishing (and Dogs)." It's a breathtaking work. And while clearly about hunting, fishing (and dogs), it's more so about time, how you choose to spend it, and in what environment. It's about mindfulness and being present. Like Harrison, I find myself becoming more conscious of my time, my environments, and my company. It is, I suppose, both the luxury and the curse of growing older.

"What are the peculiar landscapes of mind that fueled the decisions behind how I lived my life, and what were the largely unconscious impulses?" Harrison ponders. *"When you map your life in retrospect, there's a bit of a blind cartographer at work. It's not pleasurable but you have to see the structure of the way you spend your hours as a palimpsest of time overlaying the whole brutish structure, a four-dimensional topographical map with the fourth dimension being time. Simply enough, what did I do with my time?*

"I mean the life outside the dominating forces of your work, your livelihood, the jobs that offered only in the oldest terms 'room and board'." We often, he goes on to say, *"leave out of our life the learning of skills that give us pleasure, except those tied to our livelihood.*

"Our true daylight comes when we take some time off and are doing something else radically different enough to get a clear view backwards." And only then, within that new lens, can we *"reenter the woods and rivers with a moment-by-moment sense of the glories of creation, of the natural world as a living fabric of existence, so that I'm both young again, but also seventy thousand years old."*

For outdoorsman, it's almost second nature to measure time in seasons. The fresh budding of the trees each spring. The green leaves pulling in life through the warm summer days. The slow turn of color in autumn before silently falling to the forest floor. And then cold winds blowing through bare branches in winter. Each of these seasons, in turn, is made up of immeasurable small moments. A handful of these moments live on to become the fabric of traditions, the mementos of victories and the vestiges of failures.

At 48, I'm entering the sobering autumn of my life, and over the years, I've collected a fair smattering of these mementos in the outdoors with family and a few close friends. In this season, I realize that the people and the places have become far more important to me than the fish I catch, the game I take, or the peaks I bag.

Looking down at the harvested deer, I'm grateful for another season in these woods. Where, seasons before, my dad and I walked together, my boys tumbled behind, and my dog bounded like a prisoner set free. I am grateful for the quiet that allows reentry into life with a moment-by-moment sense of the glories of creation. I'm grateful to feel young again but also older, a little wiser, and more present.

With the six-point carefully hung on the camp buckpole, we're out in the barn gathered around the sawmill. Cigarette smoke hangs heavy in the cold air. The large fallen beech is running through, inches at a time. The blade is loud, almost feral. We can't talk. Instead, like Leopold, we watch sawdust fall in fragrant chips of history, mesmerized. Inch by inch, exposing a long, cross-sectioned plank that will become a table where meals will be shared and stories will be told. We splash water over the top and then a quick wipe of the hand to expose the grain. The blemishes and flaws marking its beauty.

And only then does it strike me how much this old tree is like my own life. Oftentimes, I find myself measuring moments in terms of the crosscut. I find myself counting the rings, reducing the view to a numeric value. But when the tree is cut lengthwise, a much more robust picture takes shape. Like this tree, a life is not made up of linear rings, counting years, but rather the long cut, revealing both beauty and blemish over decades. The true grain of an existence.

With the din of the saw now silenced, I once again hear the echo of the forest. The past and the present melding as one; the beauty and blemishes. And I am alive.

Pink Cake

It was the end of opening day at camp. The wood stove was glowing, and we were all gathered around the old table after dinner. The stories of the hunt growing taller as the drinks grow shorter. Dogs stirred restlessly around our feet. Jeff slowly opened the container his wife had sent along to reveal the cake. Pink cake, specifically. Covered in pink frosting. With some sprinkly shit on top for good measure and a note that read: *"Enjoy deer camp, boys. Love Julie."*

We all, of course, wanted cake. But it was pink. With pink frosting. And that sprinkly shit. Eventually, masculine pride succumbed to the draw of something sweet. Turns out pink cake is downright delicious, and I don't know what those sprinkles were made of, but I suspect they are a near cousin to

Pink Cake

cocaine.

What started out as a joke has developed into a cherished opening-day deer camp tradition. After every opening-day meal since that first time, we eat pink cake on real plates; the victorious get first dibs. It's not allowed to be touched before. That would be bad luck. Everyone knows it. It sits temptingly on the counter until the allotted time.

Our group gathers every year at my buddy's log cabin in upper Michigan. It has hosted some form of deer camp for the last thirty years running. Butch and a few of his family and friends built it by hand on the top of a pine-covered hill with a sweeping view. Before the cabin, they slept in Army hammocks in a pole barn with dirt floors and a yard-sale wood stove. If the walls could talk, well, let's just say it might not be suitable for all ages. There are stories. And traditions. Pink cake is one of them, at least now.

We hunt the vast public hills just across the street. Each area with a name inherited over time. The Pipe Stand. The Ridge. The Honey Hole. The Sniper's Nest. Each unique. Each special to one in the group. Each with a hundred stories.

Over the years, the camp roster has evolved. At first it was Butch and his parents and brother. Over time, a few of the friends joined in. I cut in maybe fifteen or twenty years ago now; I've honestly lost track. My entry into the club was through my best friend, Jeff (the bearer of the cake), who I've known since Little League days. Camp now includes some of our kids, my dad, and sometimes even my cousin.

It's hard to put into words how special that place and that time is. I, of course, remember the deer we've taken over the years, although more and more I need the photos to jog the memory. *What year was that again? Was that 2011 or 2012? Oh yeah, that was the year of the triple sevens.* More than the deer I remember time with my buddies tramping through the woods, tracking, dragging, getting lost, getting in fights, drinking, shooting, driving the old two tracks, swapping stories, playing cards, assembling stands, cutting down trees, splitting wood, sitting by fires, and staring at the stars in a vain attempt to predict the next day's weather. It all sounds pretty simple. And it is, really. And that, I suppose, is the beauty.

The best parts of life are made up of these, the small moments with family and friends. New places to explore and warm coffee from an old thermos. Cheap beer and good bourbon. Stories around the wood stove and cards around the table, where earlier we gathered for dinner after bowing our heads to give thanks. It's about traditions passed from one generation to the next — like pink cake at the end of a cold November day, sprinkly shit and all. It's the unwarranted blessings of life and health to enjoy another season, and the anticipation for the next that begins before the last bite of cake is gone.

FOOTPRINTS

We cut our first elk tracks five miles in, post-holing through heavy snow past the knee. Kyle has taken the front, breaking the trail, one foot slowly in front of the other. A faint *whoomph-and-crunch* with every step. Despite the cold, I'm sweating from exertion. A gust of wind howls over the saddle. Flipping up my hood, I watch the sun burn off the last morning clouds. It's the first full day of the hunt. I squint from the sunlight and the grin that creases my face. I could not imagine a more perfect moment.

This trip has been two years in the making — a D.I.Y. backcountry public-land hunt in Montana with my oldest son, Kyle, who is a student here. Since the idea first took hold, I have been plotting, planning, scouting, training, shooting, upgrading equipment, and packing for this very moment. And now, after a long twenty-six-hour drive, I am living it. Here, with him, in our element.

I catch my breath and do my best to follow the size-twelve boot prints. Deeper into the heart of the beckoning wilderness. Deeper into the new, yet seemingly familiar, landscape that binds us. Briefly I'm reminded of a Theodore Roosevelt quote from his book, *Wilderness Hunter*: "*Day in and day out we plodded on. In a hunting trip the days of long monotony in getting to the ground, and the days of unrequited toil after it has been reached, always far outnumber the red-letter days of success. But it is just these times of failure that really test a hunter. In the long run, common sense and dogged perseverance avail him more than any other qualities...*"

Surely this is what our 26th President envisioned when he penned those words.

Back at camp, we build a campfire and cook up eggs with ground venison and taco seasoning. This concoction is then thrown on hot dog buns and covered in Ketchup before being washed down with cold beer. We dub them "Crater Dogs." Everything, they say, tastes better in the mountains, even this. Especially after ten hard miles in tough terrain. Looking at his plate, Kyle laughs, recalling some of the more creative dishes we've eaten over the years. He brings up Mentos candy at an early deer camp. They had frozen overnight, and he chipped his tooth trying to eat them. I feel myself grinning stupidly at the memory. If his mother only knew. But Kyle learned early on the sacred credo that what happens at deer camp stays at deer camp. Tired, we watch the embers burn down as we talk about the day, reminisce about campfires past, and lay our plans for tomorrow before finally turning in.

The next morning, we're off to a new location, up well before the sun. Once again, I find myself following his lead. A steep game trail leads over the first cliff, crests one false summit and then another before reaching the glassing spot overlooking a deep and wrinkled drainage. The scent of sagebrush and evergreen hang gently on a faint breeze. Behind the mountains, the sky is beginning to glow, like a just-lit lantern. As the first streaks of dawn grow gradually brighter, Kyle spots the day's first deer. A group of seven brown spots off to the left. He keeps watch as I continue to glass the rest of the bowl. And then his clenched whisper breaks the silence: "*Buck!*" The words stab like electricity through my body. Looking over, I see four more deer have joined the group, and one clearly is wearing headgear. The rangefinder reads just over 300, a little longer than I'd prefer. I pull up the .30-06 to take a closer look. A tall fork and three does. I want to take this buck. A small argument ensues. Reluctantly the gun drops. Junior has talked me down. After all, he assures me, we have many more days to come. Eventually, the deer work up and over the hill and quietly vanish into the broken landscape as if mere figments of our imagination. For now, the rifle remains silent.

In the moment, I'm reminded of one of our first hunts together. We're in tree stands, maybe ten yards apart, hunting whitetail in northern Michigan. I can still picture him, small in his oversized camo with the legs rolled up and his giant boots. The anticipation fresh in his young eyes as the morning dawns. I spotted the first buck and caught Kyle's attention, pointing to my eyes and then in the direction of the activity. He acknowledges the signal and tenses. The deer crosses through but never comes into range. Not long after, a second buck meanders through the thick vegetation before we can set up for a shot. The disappointment is palpable. We wait a little longer. There's more movement. A small six point moves down the run coming into range. We make eye contact knowingly. Kyle draws back, and as the buck crosses into the shooting lane, I give a quick grunt that stops him. My heart is in my throat. My eyes only on the deer. I hear the arrow release as the buck runs off. The shot falling safely short. Glancing over I can see the frustration, the tears welling up. This, I assure him, is hunting. There will be more misses. More frustrations. More mistakes. I talk him down.

We've decided to pack up camp and drive southeast about four hours to an entirely new location where last year Kyle filled his tag on a giant muley. We leave the snow and the mountains in the rearview and head deeper and deeper into an arid landscape that is both beautiful and bizarrely different. One filled with history and conflict. An almost desert-like

Footprints

terrain with rolling hills, strange rock formations, and steep cliffs with draw after draw. We make camp for the night, build our fire, and dig through the cooler for something to call the evening's dinner. Coyotes bid a distant goodnight before we extinguish the lantern.

Kyle has promised to take me to the spot he shot his buck last year, an overlooked section of BLM property that borders state land. The weather is pleasant and the wind perfect. We settle in with anticipation. It feels special, seeing this place. Somehow sacred; a glimpse into part of his world that I wasn't there for. A watershed moment for him as a hunter and a man. He methodically walks through the sequence of events from last season and watch it unfold like I was there. The buck coming down the draw. The anxiety as he plays the wind, moves into position, and waits on the shot. The excitement of the trigger pull and the momentary disbelief when the buck falls. The mix of joy and sorrow that comes from taking the life. The warmth of the animal as he first lays hands on him. The coyotes howling nearby as he quarters out the meat, and the weight biting into his shoulders on the pack out. It's a hell of a story, and I have to choke back a bit of fatherly pride that comes with hearing it.

Despite perfect conditions, there's little activity. For a couple hours, we simply sit and talk and laugh quietly. Sharing stories of past hunts. Remembering adventures together. Fishing, camping, hunting, girls, school, family, places, life.

For the first time in a while, I'm completely present. Removed from distractions in a way only places like this can afford. He recalls one of the first times he came afield with me, he and his younger brother. I had my bow, and we crept along together until we spotted a few does. Me in front with the boys following eagerly behind. Kyle remembers, very vividly, me getting upset (at least to a young child's mind) about him stepping on a branch while we were on the stalk. Apparently, it left an impression because he always chooses his steps carefully now.

Suddenly, in the timber to the left, there's movement. The pulse once again quickens, snapped back to the present. I range the spot at 240, pull up the rifle and wait. I see legs through the tress. Could we actually have a repeat right here in this very spot? I wait for the buck to walk out.

But then into the opening, as if by some sleight of hand, a lone bull appears. Large. I can hear my own heartbeat. Kyle and I steal glances at each other. He mouths the words, *"He's huge!"* The bull crosses directly through where Kyle's buck fell last season. Broadside. He turns his head, and we can see the full width of his antlers now. I find myself holding my breath. He's easily 300 inches, with dark beams and stark white tips. For a moment, time feels frozen. My brain feels three steps behind.

In this unit, our tags aren't good for an elk on federal land, and on state land they can only be used on a spike bull or cow.

This bull is alone and moving toward the state-land border. We decide, perhaps just to see if we can, to drop back over the ridge, play the wind and see if we can loop around and intersect him on the state property — who knows what might happen. We leave everything except the guns and, once over the safety of the ridge, nearly sprint to work a cutoff. Kyle leads the way, masterfully avoiding sticks that might betray our presence. Carefully crossing the barbed wire that designates the border, we crest a ridge and watch an opening. Within moments, the bull comes into the shooting lane and stands broadside at 200 yards. We have him dead to rights, if we only had the tags. He pauses a moment and then slowly trots off as daylight begins to fade. We look at each other and shake our heads in disbelief. It's hard to comprehend the sequence of events that just unfolded. We both know we had him — and we did it together.

    Darkness settles in, and Kyle can't find his headlamp; so I take the lead while he guides from the back. We grab the packs and make the long trek back to camp. Finally, the tent comes into view, and I breathe a sigh of relief. I'm tired and hungry, but Kyle is frantic. Now he can't find his hat. He had placed it in his pocket when we were chasing down the bull and here, back at camp, it's gone. I'm annoyed, but he reminds me that this isn't just any hat, this was my hat that I gave him to use when he was six and never got back. This is the hat that has been on his head for every successful hunt he's ever undertaken.

He can think of nothing else. We tear camp apart. The tent, the truck, the duffels, the storage bin, everything. But we both know the hat is likely somewhere back in the dark. Lost along the crazy route we just navigated over the last two hours. He wants to search, but we realize it's a needle in a haystack. Tomorrow morning is our last hunt, but, knowing the power of lucky hats, I promise him we will go look before we pack up.

The last morning is a Hail Mary. We sit until shooting light and then move to a small ridge overlooking a large basin. We're more aggressive in our approach. Time is not on our side. Kyle is in front and crests the top just a bit too quickly. There are deer, but we've bumped them. I hold the scope on the saddle they will cross at 320, and a decent buck passes into the crosshairs. I hold the shot. In many ways, I just don't want the finality of the adventure. For the hunt to be finished. To have this time with my son end. We pursue them over the top, but they have vanished as quickly as the years since Kyle and I started hunting together. There's a lump in my throat at the thought.

After packing up, as promised, I agree to retrace our steps in search of the beloved hat. From camp, we cross through a meadow and then drop into a drainage where, in the dark, we followed an old cow trail the night before. Another half mile and still no sign. We follow our footprints from the evening before and the tracks of a lone coyote that must have passed through not long after we did. I'm discouraged but not surprised. We are, after all, looking for a camouflaged hat in the middle of a timbered forest. Kyle won't be dissuaded. He moves on ahead, and I follow. Suddenly, he stops and points. And there, lying beside the path is his hat. I don't know if I'm surprised or relieved or grateful — likely a cocktail of all three. The hat has been retrieved and with it, all the memories it holds. He slips it on, and we hike out in silence. It's time to head home.

We hunted hard to the very last minute, putting over forty miles on the boots and pack over six days, through rugged and breathtaking terrain. But in the end, the tags went unfilled. And while I longed to wrap my hands around battle-scarred antlers, feel the heft of a heavy pack on the shoulders, and cook fresh tenderloins over a campfire, I found myself, surprisingly, not disappointed in the experience. I had gotten what I came for: time with my son doing what we love, together outside in the backcountry. We had the opportunity to test ourselves. To reminisce about previous adventures. To share laughs around campfires. To breathe in sage-tinted air and once again feel wild and alive. And it gave me something to look forward to, another excuse to come back. An unfinished chapter in the book.

Kyle wrote this: *"On the car ride back, my dad turned and asked me what my favorite part of the week was. Initially I said it was the night we successfully spotted and stalked a 300-inch bull to within 200 yards. But that wasn't it. My favorite part was watching my love* for the outdoors come full circle.

"For 18 years my dad has been by my side nearly every time I stepped into the outdoors for an adventure. Whether it was hunting, fishing, camping or everything in between, my dad was by my side, guiding me, coaching me, or exploring with me. But this time it was different. This time the roles were reversed.

"That, I realized, was truly my favorite part. For the first time in my life I was able to guide and coach my father while we both explored the Montana wilderness. Although I enjoyed every minute of our hunt together, the whole time I couldn't help but acknowledge that neither of us would be standing there together if it wasn't for the deep appreciation for the outdoors that he had long instilled in me at a young age."

I simply don't believe anything could make a father's heart fuller than those words.

What I brought home can't be clutched in the hand, but it is possessed nonetheless — the burning for adventure, the thirst for wild places, the contentment in my soul only found in nature, and, more than anything else, the memories of irreplaceable moments with my son.

I miss the little boy in the oversized camo and the borrowed hat. I miss the times he followed in my footsteps sometimes carelessly stepping on sticks. But today I couldn't be prouder to follow *his* footprints on the path that leads deep into a wilderness we both love.

BANANAS IN THE BOAT

I'm a newbie to the world of upland hunting, and right out of the gate, I make a rookie mistake, asking Jon about his dog on our drive north. He tries his best to answer cryptically without directly saying anything positive about Winston, lest our day be cursed before we even get started.

But I can tell I have seriously stepped in it. Quickly changing the subject, I attempt to scrape as much of the bad voodoo off the bottom of my boots as possible. The truck already has an odor I can almost taste. And I see myself as he must see me right now — that buddy eagerly ready to board my drift boat, rod in one hand and banana in the other, camo neoprene waders strapped tight. Yep. I'm now that guy.

At this point, we have two choices: turn around and call it

a day; or endure the bird-less hunt I have doomed us to, hoping it exorcises the demons for next time. We elect the latter and take our lumps, going zero for six while Rod Stewart croons *"I ain't superstitious but a black cat crossed my trail"* on a continuous loop in my head.

Bragging up a bird dog prior to a hunt has now been added to the list of what many non-believers call "superstitions." But those of us who have experienced bird-less, fish-less, and game-less days know these are much more than a forgivable faux pas — these are grievous gaffes and deplorable day-wreckers.

I have a rifle that I know for a fact is cursed. Not that it can't shoot. At the range, it's a tack driver at two hundred yards, round after round after round. And I have never missed an animal with it, because I have never seen an animal when I have it with me. Oh, I've taken plenty of game with every other rifle I have ever owned; several with the .308, both .30-06s and .243s, and even the trusty .30-30, but *never* the .270. And, like a banana on a boat, its bad luck has now spread beyond me to my entire camp. Deer-less sits will oftentimes lead to frantic searches among friends and family for the .270. "Where is it?" they demand accusingly, tearing apart the truck and cabin to find the guilty culprit. All the while I feign innocence, knowing I have smuggled the offender along in a vain attempt to break the curse. For now, the gun's only value is as a threat to my boys that one of them — whomever treats me badly — will be bequeathed this sanity-sapping safe queen upon my demise.

Fly rods are the same. Any fool knows you can only fish even-numbered rods successfully. Sure, I own fives and sevens, but they are purely show pieces to fill out the collection, they don't actually see time on the water. Because they don't catch fish. I always pretend to give them consideration, but it's a fool's errand. And I round up or down when even remotely considering the five-weight — the most expensive setup in my entire assemblage. Surely the four will be enough or, better yet, I'll size up to the six, oh heck, why not just go with the eight. In fly fishing, bad luck comes in odd numbers.

Or how about flies? I have boxes and boxes and boxes of flies. I don't even dare tally the dollar value. And yet, I find myself fishing the same two or three over and over. Because they are lucky. They produce. I've lost count of the near-death experiences encountered while recovering these precious pieces of feather, fur, and yarn from precarious mishaps. Over the waders in swift current while standing on tip toes and pulling down branches? Check. Completely submerged, diving into a log jam to free the captive? Check. Hell, I would abandon the boat to save the fly. Every. Damn. Time. And then there are, of course, those friends who try to talk down the luck. Impart wisdom like, "You catch the most fish with that fly because you fish it most often." And I'll admit to giving these brash accusations brief consideration. I'll turn them around in my head for a bit. *Do I actually fish the fly more often because it catches more fish, or does it catch more fish because I fish it more often?* These thoughts keep me awake at night, my local party-store cashier employed, and my shrink's kid in an Ivy League school.

And don't even get me started on lucky hats. The most potent of all talismans, the lucky hat is not to be trifled with. I have, well *had*, two absolute workhorses in the lucky hat department. I mean the can't-miss, guaranteed-to-produce variety. The alpha, the king of the coat rack, was a battered old veteran that had become a signature. A staple on all successful fishing outings. This year, I brought him along to explore some new water with a couple of buddies. Things took a bit of a tailspin that involved our raft raking hard through a sweeper. First head on. Then sideways. Then backwards. Somehow all souls on board survived. Every rod was intact. Every pair of sunglasses accounted for. But the ol' vet was nowhere to be found. Taken before his time to a watery grave along a river that gave up no fish. My season took a turn for the worse at that point, the relievers doing their best to get me through the tough late innings. I seriously considered giving up fishing entirely. Maybe something easy like golf or pickleball instead. I never even had a chance for a proper goodbye.

Jon drops me back at my truck, barely slowing before throwing my gear out as quickly as possible while mumbling a half-hearted, "We should do this again some time," and beating a hasty retreat. "You bet," I say holding my bag bewilderedly while taillights wink off into the dusky night.

And now I sit by the phone, waiting for a call that I know isn't coming, considering who might be dumb enough to buy that five-weight or the cursed .270 and Googling recipes for banana bread I can only hope to offer in apology.

Season's End

Maybe I'm just a romantic at heart or maybe it's my age. For whatever reason, I find myself drawn to old things and old places. Authentic places. Places with stories. Places you can feel.

The North Branch Outing Club is one of those places. Over a century of history abides within these walls and along the well-worn paths lining the river's edge. It's easy to imagine the dining room bustling with elegantly dressed visitors from all over the world, traveling by rail and coach to this quiet northern Michigan respite. Or to summon mental images of the person who might have rested on this very bench and contemplated their fly selection, or in this chair by the fireplace with a book. In the library, if you listen close enough, you can almost hear the conversations and feel the presence of those who came before.

Or maybe it's just the season. It's a moody, overcast, early November day, and the place is nearly empty as the staff begins the shut down for the coming winter. The first wet snow of the year is starting to fall. I pour a cup of coffee from the dinged-up thermos and take my time pulling on the waders. There's no rush.

The breeze carries the scent of wet leaves with just a hint of what's to come. Like the smell of an old book or wood burning in a fireplace, it's familiar and comforting. I take a sip of the coffee and watch the old bird dog lounge in front of the door. The sun peaks through the clouds and, for a moment, the trees are covered in a dappled light.

I finish the coffee and slowly pull up the waders to make my way down to the river, the old hunting dog following lazily behind. The breeze brushes my neck, and I flip up my collar with an involuntary shiver.

The Au Sable is a quiet river and even more so on a day like today. I gently step in, and, as the water parts around my feet, I stop for a moment, feeling nostalgic for a slower, simpler, and more elegant time.

Winter

A hollow wind rattles
Through bare branches, while new white
Hangs on pine boughs like Christmas cookie frosting.
The old wool cruiser, musty with pipe tobacco and gun oil.
Leaving the woodstove, brisk air cuts at my face.
I flip up the collar and break fresh tracks.
It's winter…

DOG YEARS

Sunday morning walks in the woods have always been our routine. And somehow, she always knows what day of the week it is. Some unknown tell. Some mysterious divination. She won't leave my side until she's safely loaded into the back of the 4runner. And she'll shake and cry until I finally unlatch the grated door that stands between her and the trail.

She's 12, or 84 in people years, yet still gets excited about these walks. She can't jump up into her travel crate anymore, so I lift her in. And she's maybe not quite as fast as she used to be, but still surprising when she decides to be. She'll find a warm spot in the sun coming through the front door to nap when we get back, but she always gives a hundred percent when we hike.

I've always thought of our walks as me doing something for her, but more and more, I wonder if she does it for me. Recognition of an unspoken need.

I still remember the first time we met. A litter of nine pups — eight males, one female. A writhing mass of puppiness. She was so small; the runt. And very white with much less ticking than her brothers. She saw us, climbed the barrier of the puppy box, and boldly walked up to me. I picked her up in one hand and held her up to my face. She proceeded to bite my nose and then quickly lick it, in half-hearted apology. I knew this was my dog. A Christmas present for our boys twelve years ago. They were just five and seven.

Now I notice the grey around her muzzle and wonder if she notices the silver around my temples. I can't bear the thought — won't allow myself to think about it — but I know our time together grows shorter and shorter and I'll likely be the one saying a tearful goodbye.

Dog years. Like people years, but poignantly compressed. We've had so many walks together that I've barely noticed as the time has passed.

I just sent my oldest back to college in Montana after the holidays, and my youngest graduates next year. My closest friend since childhood just crossed the midway mark of his forties, and 2019 marked twenty-five years of marriage and twenty years owning my business.

The days of wide-eyed kids opening presents by the tree

while a puppy plays with the wrappings lay behind me. But I feel blessed by another Sunday morning walk with my dog, who to me will always remain a puppy, and the joy of another holiday season with family and friends who in my mind remain forever young.

Afterword

One Last Walk

We're heading into the wooded grove that has been our go-to spot for so many Sunday outings. The place I learned to hunt as a boy, and where you worked tirelessly as a younger dog, always circling back to ensure I was keeping up. Thirteen seasons, in all kinds of weather. For all kinds of reasons. Or sometimes no reason at all. Our secret place of escape where we run free. It's warmer than usual, and I'm sweating, longing for the coolness of the creek bottom where we always begin.

I navigate the bank and instinctively look ahead for your white body flashing through the forested landscape. Bounding. Carefree. Following your nose. I start to give a quick whistle to call you back, only then remembering that this last time you aren't running. You're in a small tin I carry awkwardly in my arms.

Glancing down, I'm forced to face the reality that you are actually gone. Your graceful, muscular frame, mischievous brown eyes, and bobbed tail that followed you like an exclamation point, reduced to dusty ashes in a box. My eyes blur and burn from stains of sadness that leach in long salty streaks down my face and fall in futile silence on my shirt and the dry forest floor.

This was where I thought I'd lay you for your final rest. The creek where you chased fish and retrieved rocks. Where you'd cool down and grab a quick drink before tearing off again. But now it doesn't feel right. Too permanent. Not enough. Maybe no place ever will be, or maybe I just can't bring myself to let go completely.

It was unbearable to watch as the cancer slowly ate you away. A black demon inside I was powerless to exorcise. An uninvited guest unwilling to leave. Somehow this day always seemed so far off. But your thinning body, skin hung like a suitcoat too big for a child on your frame, and the telltale arch in your back belying the pain you hid so well told the story I was reluctant to hear. Somehow, you'd always rally enough for our walks. Our ritual. You'd put on a brave face and follow faithfully along. Slower than before, but always willing.

I remember finally making that call to the vet. To come and give you the peace you earned after all these loyal years. To take away the pain you hid so well. In our home.

Comfortable. Together. I remember hanging up the phone, closing my office door, and crying uncontrollably. Ugly, embarrassing crying. And I remember the day before that visit, coming to this very place together. You alongside, windows down, and ears blowing in the wind. Smiling. I swear to God you were smiling. A couple cheeseburgers for both of us on the way, because why the hell not. And then letting you go to wander. Still knowing the way. Years of walks engrained in the marrow of your bones. To fetch rocks in the creek, run in the woods, and take one last swim in the river.

There's a quote that reads "It's the last greatest thing we're able to do for a faithful friend." And I know it was, but I can't help feeling that I somehow betrayed you lying on your bed while I gently stroked your soft brown ears, shuddering as your chest heaved its last breath and your faithful heart fell silent. Feeling your warm wet tongue one final time on my hand; a small reassurance that left a hole impossible to fill back in.

Climbing out of the creek bottom, we move on. Toward the overlook by the river. Where we'd always stop for a spell. I'd sit and watch the river while you fetched sticks. Small gifts you'd bring to foot while not so patiently waiting for me to throw them again. Over and over; it never got old. But *we* did. I can feel it. In my battered body and sorrowed soul. I sense it holding thirteen years of memories in this tiny box. Even the landscape seems to have aged in a way I notice for the first time.

One Last Walk

I remember you as a puppy. God, you were a spitfire. Climbing fences, running fast on those too-long-for-your-body legs. Getting into mischief. I could never get mad. You had me completely. Sure, I'd pretend to be upset, but deep down I just chuckled when you'd flash that forlorn look at me. Those sad eyes. Ears down. I knew it was a ruse. Hell, we both did, but I played along. And I grew to love you even more as an older dog. Maybe we just came to understand each other better in those years.

I sit for a while at the overlook, watching the river far below. Reliving our walks together. The memories temporarily lighten the moment, but glancing down at the small tin by my side, I'm heavy again. There's a lump in my throat I can't swallow. A grief that feels bottomless has overtaken me. My buddy Jon told me, "Every dog takes a piece of us with them, which is partly why it's so hard to let them go." I fear in letting you go you're taking the better parts of me with you. The happy me. The younger me. The me that runs free in these woods. Leaving just the husk. Rattling and empty. But those are selfish thoughts. I wipe my cheek and reluctantly pour out your ashes, releasing you for the last time into the wind and woods and water you so loved.

Then I walk back to the truck. Numb. Unsure of the moment. Empty container in hand; a stark reflection of the hollowness that has overtaken me. What I wouldn't give to have you alongside just one more time.

Back home, I walk through the door still expecting you to greet me, as was our routine. I'm met instead by the sight of your leash and collar hanging pensively on the coatrack.

I choke back another wave of tears and remember our walks. At that moment, I finally realize that while you took an enormous piece of me with you, you left some pieces of yourself for me too. And while our time together seemed so unjustly short, I will never walk in the woods without you by my side.

And today, that will have to be enough.

Lucy
November 1, 2007 – July 2, 2021

About the Author

Allen is a husband and father of two sons who frequently out-hunt and out-fish him. He is President and part owner of an advertising agency located in Michigan and an active member of Trout Unlimited, Backcountry Hunters and Anglers, and the Michigan Outdoor Writer's Association. He is a frequent podcast guest and runs a blog, *allenoutside.com*, dedicated to outdoor pursuits.

Allen is a bibliophile with a weakness for books about everything — but especially travel, adventure, war, history, and outdoor pursuits. He loves great food, great bourbon, and great wine, sometimes in moderation, sometimes not.

More than anything, he loves the outdoors — the smells, the sounds, the sights. Since he was a little boy fishing with his dad, pitching a tent in the backyard, and unwrapping pocketknives for Christmas, he's been drawn to all things wild.

Made in the USA
Monee, IL
04 February 2023